A MURDER
IN
AMISH OHIO

A MURDER
IN
AMISH OHIO

The Martyrdom of Paul Coblentz

DAVID MEYERS AND ELISE MEYERS WALKER

THE
History
PRESS

ACKNOWLEDGEMENTS

W hile researching this story, we incurred a debt of gratitude to many people, but we would like to specifically recognize the following: Sergeant Maria Stryker, Holmes County Sheriff's Office; Ginnie Sandison, Holmes County Clerk of Courts; Martin Yant, Ace Investigations; Teresa Carstensen, Ohio History Connection; Abraham Hochstetler, AmishAbe.com; Licensed Private Investigator Teresa Edwards; Sheriff Steve Sloan, Stark County, Illinois; Marynell Reardon, Wooster Historical Society; Candace Barnhart and Gwen Uhl, Holmes County Historical Society; Guy Roy Stallman, Holmesville; John Rodrigue, The History Press; Amy Gerber Doerfler; Abraham Hochstetler; Ron Miller; Mary Lou Kunkler; Randy McNutt; Nathan Weaver; Beverly Meyers; and Mike Dumoulin. Each of them contributed in some way to the finished product.

We also would like to thank the Grandview Heights Library, Cleveland Public Library, Library of Congress, Holmes County Clerk of Courts and others as noted for the use of specific images. It is becoming increasingly difficult for authors to obtain good images without paying an arm and a leg for the right to reproduce them. Most of us are simply trying to break even, let alone turn a profit on our books. So we are grateful for those institutions that recognize that fact.

While the Amish use the Luther Bible, which was translated into German from Hebrew and ancient Greek by Martin Luther, all biblical quotes are from the King James version.

INTRODUCTION

Every man must give an account of himself to God, and therefore every man ought to be at liberty to serve God in that way that he can best reconcile to his conscience.
—*John Leland*[1]

In the summer of 1957, a farmer was murdered in Holmes County, Ohio. There was little to distinguish this slaying from hundreds of others that occurred throughout the United States that year except for the ethnicity of the victim. He was Amish. As sensational crimes often do, it opened a window into the private lives of the young man, his family and his community—a community that, in some respects, remains as enigmatic today as it was more than half a century ago.

For many Americans, the "Amish murder" was a revelation. Unless they lived in rural parts of Ohio, Pennsylvania, Indiana or a few other states, they may not have had any exposure to these "peculiar people" with their "plain" manner of dress and their "simple" lifestyle. Even if they did, it was unlikely they knew them well. The Amish tend to keep to their own kind, having intentionally withdrawn from the larger society—from the "world." At least, they try. But sometimes the world won't be denied.

For years, Lancaster County, Pennsylvania, has been known as the heart of Pennsylvania Dutch country—"Pennsylvania Dutch" being a shorthand term for the descendants of early German-speaking immigrants. This included such religious groups as Lutheran, German Reformed, Moravian, Schwarzenau Brethren ("Dunkards"), Mennonite and Amish. After *National*

One of a series of WPA posters that promoted Pennsylvania tourism. *Library of Congress.*

Geographic magazine published an article about the region in 1938, many East Coast city-dwellers were prompted to make an occasional excursion there. And by 1955, roughly twenty-five thousand people per year were visiting Lancaster County. Sixty-five years later, that number tops 8 million.

Holmes County, Ohio, by contrast, had virtually no tourism to speak of back then and continues to lag well behind Lancaster County. Despite being the locus of the largest Amish settlement in the world, it has about half as many visitors. As sociologist Donald Kraybill observed, "In 1957, Amish-themed tourism was still in its infancy and few Americans even knew of the Amish, let alone anything about their culture and beliefs, so journalists arriving in rural Holmes County struggled to interpret the story for their readers."[2]

For many, reader and reporter alike, it might as well have been a foreign country. Different customs, different lifestyle, different manner of dress and even a different language: Pennsylvania German. It was like stepping back in time. But what they found particularly puzzling was that the Amish expressed no hatred toward the killers and no desire for retribution. To quote one Amish man, "We do not engage in revenge; that is for God."[3]

Incredibly, the Amish seemed to be as concerned about helping the perpetrators and their families get through the sad ordeal as they were the victim's family and themselves. So they prayed for them, hoping that God would forgive their sins. And they reached out to them, inviting the parents of the killers into their homes and visiting the murderer in prison, before returning to the privacy of their own families and community.

There was a similar reaction nearly fifty years later when ten Amish girls between the ages of six and thirteen were gunned down on October 2, 2006, at a schoolhouse in Nickel Mines, Pennsylvania. Five of the victims died, and five others were wounded when a local milk truck driver barged into their one-room school and shot the children in cold blood. The world was horrified and then astounded—horrified by the senseless slaughter of innocent little girls and astounded that the Amish community again responded not with anger, but forgiveness.

Although grief-stricken by their loss, the Amish reached out to the family of the gunman, recognizing that his widow and children were grieving, too, and were victims as well. The Amish community would have willingly cooperated with the judicial system only to the extent necessary to allow it to carry out its function, just as they had back in 1957. However, in 2006, there was no trial because the shooter took his own life. A half century before, there were two—both for murder.

According to Howard Goeringer, a specialist in nonviolence, "Amish culture is embedded in the German word 'Gelassenheit.' It means submission, self-surrender, yielding humbly to the sovereignty of God and trusting in the Holy One's power to deliver His children from evil and death."[4] Under this doctrine, the Amish are prohibited from engaging in "ruthless competition and aggressive confrontation expressed in divorce, lawsuits, domestic violence, war, and the like."[5] For the most part, they do not look to the court system for redress, although they are appreciative of the government's efforts to keep them safe.

Because the Amish are not an immutable group, a little bit of knowledge about them is almost as bad as none. The original church has subdivided many times over the centuries due to doctrinal disputes. The Coblentz family, whose son, Paul, was slain, were Old Order Amish. They are at the conservative end of the Amish spectrum, just a tad more liberal than the Andy Weaver Amish (or "Dan church") and still farther removed from the extreme right Swartzentruber Amish—"the plainest of the 'Plain People,'" to quote anthropologist Karen Johnson-Weiner.[6] Within these larger groups, there are numerous church districts, each overseen by a bishop. But beyond that, there is little in the way of formal organizational structure.

Since their arrival in the United States 250 years ago, few Amish are known to have been murdered—either by outsiders or by other Amish. However, in 2009, a Mennonite woman who was having an affair with a member of the Andy Weaver affiliation shot her lover's wife to death as she was sleeping. This occurred in Apple Creek, Ohio, roughly ten miles from the Coblentz home.

It likely came as no surprise that the husband was complicit in the crime. Twice during his ten-year marriage he had left has family to live as the "English"—the Amish term for non-Amish people. But both times, he repented of his sins and was taken back by both his church and his wife in the spirit of forgiveness. However, he then recruited the Mennonite woman—who was one of several lovers he had taken—to commit the murder.

Owing to the troubled state of her marriage, the Amish wife had consulted a counselor. In one of the last letters to her counselor, she wrote of her husband, "I often think of Christ's words. 'Forgive him for he knows not what he does.'"[7] If death had not silenced her, she likely would have said the same thing even after she was slain. That is the Amish way.

Among the most easily recognizable ethnic groups in the country, the Amish are a large and complex subculture. Like other religious separatist groups, they are responding to the biblical injunction "Come out from among them and be yet separate, saith the Lord."[8] They aren't trying to change the world—only keep it at arm's length so they can maintain their own norms, customs and lifestyles in their individual communities. It hasn't been easy, yet the Amish continue to grow and prosper. It has been projected that the Amish in Holmes County will be in the majority by 2030.

My daughter and I have written this book in an effort to provide a glimpse into the Old Order Amish culture by focusing on those points where it intersects with our own—the culture of the "English." We chose the murder of Paul Coblentz as the vehicle because so little has been written about this particular crime, although it was arguably the key event in the twentieth century when it came to opening up the Amish way of life to outside scrutiny. In doing so, we also hope to correct some of the errors that have subsequently crept into the narrative while shedding some light on the "plain folks," as they call themselves.

Admittedly, we are outsiders looking in. But so are most people who write about the Amish. In popular media, they have been overly romanticized because of their perceived virtues or overly disparaged because of their insistence on maintaining traditional gender roles. Publicly, men are dominant, but privately it may not be that simple. "They expect to help their husbands," Johnson-Weiner has written. "[I]ndeed, the prayer covering every Amish woman wears indicates that she 'accepts the position in which God has placed her as her husband's helpmeet.'"[9]

In practice, however, the husband manages the farm (i.e., supports the family financially), while the wife manages the home, including the children and the garden. The wives typically are listed on deeds, most control the checkbook and they share in all financial decisions. Some Amish women even run their own businesses. And when it comes to church, "in many respects Old Order Amish women have greater power and status in their church communities than many 'English' or non-Amish women"—even though they cannot serve as ministers.[10]

In 1905, *Sabina, A Story of the Amish*—the first Amish romance novel—was published. Written by Helen Reimensnyder Martin, it tells the story of a pretty and (as it turns out) clairvoyant Amish maid who is "haunted by a face of strange ugliness which appears from time to time as a warning of impending disaster to herself or family."[11] Other than the Pennsylvania Dutch setting, the book has little to recommend it. However, it was a precursor to a genre of romance novels now known as "bonnet rippers" that have proliferated since the release of *Witness*, the popular Harrison Ford movie, in 1985.[12]

Many have criticized Martin for her harsh portrayal of the Amish, particularly the men, through the lens of feminism. One of them, Joseph Yoder, was prompted to write his own novel, *Rosanna of the Amish*, in reaction to Martin's work, as well as Ruth Lininger Dobson's 1937 novel *Straw in the Wind*. Published in 1940, *Rosanna* was a fictionalized and sympathetic account of his mother's life and, to some extent, his own. According to Julia Spicher Kasdorf, his biographer:

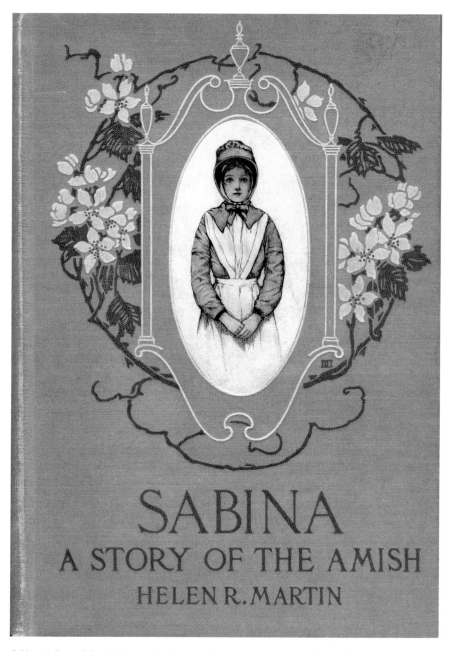

Sabina, A Story of the Amish was the first Amish romance novel. *Authors' collection.*

Yoder used Rosanna to address three commonly misrepresented areas of Amish life. First, he portrayed Bishop Shem Yoder, Rosanna's Amish stepfather, as strict but gentle instead of greedy and cruel. Second, he showed that the Amish find joy in labor and are not merely workaholics. Third, he did away with the "dumb Dutch" stereotype by making his characters astute and sensible.[13]

To be Amish is to reject *hochmut*, the German word for pride, arrogance and haughtiness, and embrace *demut*, the German word for humility. This comes at the expense of individualism. The Amish strive to submit themselves to the will of God as expressed through the group norms established by their local church. Such a stance puts them out of step with the larger American culture—deliberately so. But it also sometimes leads to confusion, misunderstanding and cultural insensitivity.

We briefly mentioned the Coblentz murder in a previous book, *Central Ohio's Historic Prisons.* To our surprise, a handful of Amish people came up to us at a book fair, picked up copies of the book and began searching through it until they found the story. As one Amish gentleman told me, the Amish do not feel it is proper to read about themselves, but they are interested in reading about other Amish. While we do not assume this volume will find a readership among the Amish, we have done our best to treat them fairly and hope they would agree.

The Amish aren't magical creatures, nor do they possess special powers. They are simply human beings. And as human beings, they are not perfect. Nor do they pretend to be. They would be the first to tell you so. Neither my daughter nor I would want to be Amish, but we are glad we live in a country that grants them the freedom to practice their faith in accordance with their conscience.

When writing about true crime, you run the risk of re-victimizing those who were most harmed during the commission of the original crime (i.e., Paul's widow, Dora, and his daughter, Esther). We know that Dora would prefer not to be discussed in this book. But we would be unable to tell the story without doing so, and we feel the story is an important one. Instead, we have withheld Dora and Esther's married names to at least provide them with that degree of anonymity. Similarly, we have omitted the names of children born to the perpetrators of the crime. We ask that you, our readers, also respect their privacy.

DAVID MEYERS

Chapter 1

THE SUMMER OF FEAR

The devil dances in an empty pocket.
—Amish proverb

Death came for Paul Coblentz about an hour before midnight on July 18, 1957. At the age of twenty-five years, seven months and nineteen days, the thread of his life was measured and cut. All that remained were a ghostly white corpse, a grieving family and too few memories. It had been as sudden as it was senseless. And it was almost unprecedented.

A young Amish farmer, Paul had retired for the night to the basement living quarters of his unfinished, one-story home. Built against a hill, it overlooked State Route 241—or Millersburg Road—an eighth of a mile away. Paul and his father, Mose, had started constructing the house three years earlier upon the publication of his marriage banns to Dora Yoder.

Together, father and son tended the family's 150-acre dairy farm.[14] Most Amish families would till less than half that amount if the ground were fertile and they weren't afraid of hard work. However, as Paul's friend and Dora's second cousin, John Miller, later wrote, "Everyone worked willingly."[15] They believed it brought them closer to God.

All that long, hot summer day, the two men had toiled in the fields harvesting wheat. Once all the grain was reaped and threshed, Mose planned to take his wife on a vacation trip out west.[16] They likely would stop to see their eldest son, Roy. In Amish families, the youngest son typically inherits the family farm, so Roy had bought a place of his own near Independence,

At the time of his death, the "little house" where Paul Coblentz and his family resided was just a basement. *Author photo.*

Iowa, where there was a large Amish settlement.[17] Two other sons had passed away. That left two daughters still living at home—and Paul.

It was Thursday night, about half past ten. At least one lamp was burning in their unimposing home. Paul was eating "a late snack of breakfast cereal," while Dora was working in the kitchen, "preparing the following day's noon meal to feed the threshing crew" that would be arriving in the morning.[18] Their infant daughter, Esther, was sleeping peacefully in the bedroom. Suddenly, the family dog started barking wildly in the yard. Awakened by the noise, Esther began crying.

As Dora went to comfort her, Paul stepped outside to investigate. Minutes later, a short man, gun in hand, entered the house. He was wearing a handkerchief tied over his mouth and nose. Dora met him in the kitchen, carrying Esther in her arms. The intruder asked the young woman if they had any horses. She replied that they did, but they had been turned out to the field for the night. He then ordered her into the living room, just off the kitchen, and told her to sit down in a rocking chair. At this point, his companion, a tall man, walked into the kitchen, holding Paul at knife point.

The intruders were "English" (i.e., non-Amish). Dora later described one of them as "almost six-feet tall and slender, wearing dark clothes and a cap similar to those worn by policemen"—by which she may have meant

Paul's empty billfold, with Dora's initials inscribed on it. *Holmes County Clerk of Courts.*

a motorcycle cap.[19] His companion was "about five feet, seven inches tall, wore dark trousers and a white T-shirt with a hunting license pinned to it."[20] He also had tattoos all over his forearms. Both smelled of alcohol, she said.

Brandishing a fish knife, the tall man directed Paul to lie face-down on the floor in the kitchen. He demanded to know where they kept their money. The young farmer told him it was in a drawer beneath the sink. The man rummaged through several drawers until he located the Amish man's leather billfold. He removed nine dollars in cash. When Paul pleaded with him not to take all of the money, he stuffed the five-dollar bill in Paul's hand and kept the four ones.

While this was occurring, the shorter man became angry with Dora and struck her in the face a number of times. He also grabbed her collar and ripped the front of her dress down to her waist, exposing her undergarments. All the while, the young mother clung to her baby. When the tall man moved to the archway between the kitchen and the living room, the two of them exchanged weapons. He handed the shorter one the knife, while he stood guard over Paul with the lever-action rifle.

Gesturing with the knife, the shorter man threatened to kill Dora's baby and her husband if she did not submit to his sexual advances. To show he was serious, he made a scratch across the baby's forehead and cut the mother on the hand. When Dora began to scream, he struck her on the head with the butt of the knife.

Sprawled out on the kitchen floor, Paul was unable to see what was happening. In desperation, he leaped to his feet and made a mad dash toward the door, presumably to summon help. Still standing in the archway, the taller man swung the rifle up to his shoulder and fired a round in the Amish man's direction. He then disappeared into the kitchen. Moments later, there was a second shot.

As soon as the shooting began, the shorter man abandoned Dora and rushed into the kitchen. Almost immediately, she followed after him. She found Paul lying halfway out the screen door in a growing pool of blood. He had been shot just behind the ear. The bullet had passed through his skull and shattered into fragments on the concrete slab beneath him. The other bullet had struck him in the lower back. Dora struggled to drag her husband back inside the house.

Seventy-five or eighty feet away, Mose and his wife, Susie, were in their own home, nestled in bed for the night. They were awakened by the dog's barks, the gunshots and Dora's screams. In Amish culture, one son takes over the farm and the main house when the father retires. A second house—the *Grossdaadi Haus* (or "grandfather's house")—is built a stone's throw away so the son can lookout after his parents in their retirement. However, Mose still occupied the main house with his wife and two daughters.

Grabbing a gasoline lantern, Mose charged out into the darkness. He immediately heard another gunshot, but whether it was intended for him or not he didn't know. It sounded like it came from a nearby lane. As his wife and daughters followed, he pushed ahead toward the crumpled form lying halfway out the door of the basement house. He saw Dora standing over Paul's body. When he realized what had happened, Mose hurried to a neighboring farm, perhaps a third of a mile away. He told the neighbor, Atlee Kauffman, to notify the authorities. Kauffman immediately ran a third of a mile farther to where there was a phone and placed a call to the Holmes County Sheriff's Office.

The "big house" where Mose Coblentz and his family lived at the time of the murder. *Author photo.*

An arrow indicates where a bullet pierced the screen door. *From the* Columbus Citizen, *Scripps-Howard Newspaper/Grandview Heights Public Library/Photohio.org*

Returning to his gravely wounded son, Mose found him unconscious but alive. Dora was dabbing at his face with wet cloths. By the time Dr. Luther W. High, acting coroner, arrived from Millersburg, however, the young man was dead. Mose's plans for the future died with him.

THE COBLENTZES BELONGED TO the Old Order Amish church. The most traditional of the Anabaptist groups—a Christian denomination that opposes the baptism of infants—they are committed pacifists.[21] They refuse to be a party to violence, aggression or resistance of any kind, even in self-defense.

Mose J. Coblentz and his wife, Susanna "Susie" E. Weaver, were married a little more than thirty years earlier on February 3, 1927, a Thursday. Most Amish wedding takes place on either a Tuesday or a Thursday and usually in the fall after the harvest season. This is because a wedding, like all things Amish, elevates the practical over any other virtue.

Susie would have worn a plain and homemade but new dress of some approved color—often blue, but never white. And her father would not have "given her away," as is common in many weddings. She and her husband-to-be would have walked through the door together. The ceremony itself is plain and simple—more like a regular Sunday service. However, up to six hundred people might participate afterward in the wedding meal.

Mose and Susie were the parents of six children—a typical family by Amish standards, in which the average number of children is seven.[22] But since the Amish do not condone birth control, some families have between ten and fifteen children, especially among the more conservative factions.

Their eldest was Roy, born on April 22, 1928. Eli followed nearly a year later on March 26, 1929, but died within the week. Jonas was next, born on December 3, 1930. He passed away on April 20, 1952, at the age of twenty-one following an asthma attack. He had been in poor health for several years, and the family had even taken him to Arizona in the hope that a change of climate would be beneficial. Paul M. was born on November 30, 1931; Katie M. on May 5, 1936; and Mary on November 4, 1944.

Not long after they started a family, Mose and Susie bought a farm near Mount Hope, several miles away. It had previously been owned by Bernice Menuez, mother of Rollin T. Menuez. Rollin was president of the Benton Bridge Company of Wooster.

Paul M. Coblentz married Dora J. Yoder on November 16, 1954, in Holmes County. Paul would have begun growing his distinctive Amish beard the day their marriage banns were posted. It is an accepted fact that Amish women usually join the church first, and Amish men join once they have found someone to marry. A few months older than her husband, Dora was born on July 11, 1931, near Fredericksburg, the daughter of John E. Yoder and Maryann N. Miller.

Although the Old Order Amish are considered conservative, in some respects they are surprisingly permissive. Take *Rumspringa*. Often mischaracterized as a period of wild and reckless behavior, *Rumspringa* ("jumping around") is actually just the term used among the Amish to describe adolescence. It ends when the young adult chooses to be baptized into to the church. Until then, some teenage rebellion is tolerated, if not encouraged.

Rumspringa is also the time when a young Amish person typically begins searching for a husband or wife—the boys at sixteen and the girls at fourteen or fifteen. Courtship exists as an open secret. The opportunities for Amish youth to interact one on one are limited. On Sunday evenings after the adults have gone home, the teenagers will generally remain at the house where the church service was held for Sunday night singing. While the singing usually ends by ten o'clock, the group will often remain an hour or two longer so that the boys and girls can talk.

According to Peter D. Lehman of Pennsylvania State University, a young man will typically initiate contact with a young women through a mutual friend. If she is receptive, they will pass messages back and forth until it is agreed that they will go on a date. "Once the two have begun dating, the boy will usually give the girl transportation home after Sunday night singings and go to see her every other Saturday night, sometimes staying into the early hours of the next morning playing games, talking, or interacting with another couple."[23]

If a couple hits it off, the boy will ask the girl if he can drive her home. Upon reaching her house, they will go in and visit. At that late hour, the household will be sleeping, so they have plenty of privacy. They may sit up late into the night getting to know each other. Afterward, the boy makes the long buggy trip home in the wee hours of the morning. If both are willing, the couple starts going steady.

The more conservative couples practice traditional Amish dating customs. They date in their open buggies and drink hot chocolate or sodas. They focus on group and outdoor activities, sometimes with their parents. Couples from more progressive churches that have drifted more toward the modern world might go into town for the evening. Maybe they will get a bite to eat or just hang out together and enjoy each other's company.

The most daring couples might change into English clothes, get into a car and head for a party, where they can sample worldly temptations. However, this group is a very small minority.

Either one can quit the relationship at any time. Just as in the outside world, it might take someone several tries to find a lifelong partner.

MOSE WAS UNDOUBTEDLY PLEASED when Paul took Dora for his wife. Because Roy had moved away and two other sons had died, Paul was his last hope. From the time they are children, the Amish are taught to care for one another. Even as the parents look after them, they are assisting with the younger children. The emphasis is on strong family ties and traditional gender roles. As they reach adulthood, the Amish frequently gather together to perform labor-intensive tasks such as harvesting crops or raising a barn. Both the men and the woman have their traditional duties to perform. When it is time, the adult children care for their parents.

A little more than a year after they married, Paul and Dora's only child, Esther, was born on December 16, 1955, in Millersburg. The couple made their home on Country Road 235—sometimes called the Township House Road—not far from the crossroads community of Mount Hope in eastern Salt Creek Township.

At twenty-five, Paul and Dora were some five or six years older than the two men who had invaded their home. Their life together had barely begun when it came to a bloody and senseless conclusion. The young widow took her child and went to live with her parents while Paul's father began planning his funeral.

According to John Miller, he and Paul were best friends at Fryburg School, and they remained close even after Paul married. When news of Paul's murder reached him, he was helping build a barn near Killbuck. Like everyone else in the Amish community, he was shocked beyond belief. Such things just didn't happen in Holmes County.

Levi Miller was a twelve-year-old Amish boy at the time of the Coblentz murder. Several nights later, he accompanied his parents to Mose Coblentz's farm for Paul's wake. A large crowd had gathered. As soon as they learned of the tragedy, the Amish community converged on the Coblentz farm to offer comfort and assistance. There were cars and buggies parked all up and down the lane.

"It was dark and there were only gas lanterns," Levi recalled, "and I remember following my parents, shaking hands with people in the front room and then ushered into a back room where the dead body lay in an open coffin for viewing with only the white face revealed by the lantern's light."[24]

As sad as it was, what Levi remembered most was the uneasiness over the whereabouts of the killers. "Were these men still hiding somewhere near one of our farms?"[25] Even after the suspects were captured, he couldn't relax. "This was the first murder I was aware of in Holmes County, and it became a summer of fear. I would look out the upstairs window, and I could not sleep, wondering if some wandering intruders may show up at our farm."[26]

Nathan Weaver's recollections echo Levi's: "The murder awoke a newfound suspicion and fear in the community where peace and trust reigned before. For the first time, seldom-locked doors were barred at night. Callers after dark needed to identify themselves before their knocks were answered. The men had intruded [upon] the whole community."[27]

To most Americans, especially in 1957, there was little understanding of what it meant to be Amish. Colonel Frank Ward, who wrote about true crime for the *Columbus Star*, covered the story. "By noon, there was a long line of the quaint rigs parked hub to hub on the hard packed drive, before a broad sweep of lawn, were interspersed with sheriffs' cruisers or highway patrol cars," noted Ward, who had hurried to the scene.[28]

> *The Amish women, in their somber garb and wearing little, white lace caps, conversed in whispers. On one end of the bench was the young widow and her child. The Amish men, all wearing beards, talked in low tones of the worst crime ever to befall their community. They wore black suits, without buttons. Their white shirts were homemade and home laundered. Their coats and vests were fastened with hooks and eyes.*[29]

The funeral was planned for Monday, July 22, in Mose's barn—a large barn, but not large enough. More than one thousand mourners were expected, arriving from all over Holmes and Wayne Counties and elsewhere. They would come by horse-drawn wagons and buggies to pay their last respects and to reinforce the shared bonds of community that united them.

In her work with the Amish, psychologist Kathleen B. Bryer observed, "The Amish people see death as a part of the natural rhythm of life, within a religious belief system based on the teachings of the New Testament the person's relationship to death as one of human temporality and divine eternity."[30]

Rebecca Miller, a member of an Old Order Amish church in Holmes County, has provided a detailed account of the preparations for a typical Amish funeral. While nearby farmers cleared the manure out of the barn with their teams, "other men cleaned out the shop where services would be held. Meanwhile, the women and girls cleaned both houses, the shop, weeded the garden, and mowed the yard."[31]

A food committee of church women would plan all the meals, compiling lists of what and how much was needed of each item and then notifying other neighboring church ladies who would prepare them. Men would haul in bench wagons from neighboring churches and begin setting them up, while a delegation of older women and family members would tend to the widow.

According to Colonel Ward, Mose Keim, a neighbor and cabinet maker, arrived and questioned Paul's "father about the weight and height of his dead son."[32] He then made a plain oak coffin and lined it with white muslin. Lacking handles, it would be carried by four pallbearers—John C. Miller,

Vernon Kline, Levi Stutzman and Elmer Miller—using six-foot-long hickory sticks. They also would dig the grave at Troyer Cemetery, a family plot one mile to the north.

Bishop John Fry would deliver the principle sermon, but other bishops and ministers would also speak and read scripture. Following the conclusion of the service, lunch would be served on the tree-shaded lawn surrounding the big white house. There would be Swiss cheese, trail bologna, potato salad, gelatin dessert, coffee, bread and jam. After the meal, they would all set out for Troyer Cemetery.

The coffin would be transported to the cemetery in a narrow horse-drawn, buckboard-type wagon supplied by Mose Keim. Those Amish in attendance would collect in a large circle about the grave and chant religious songs in German, while the earth was being shoveled into the grave by the pallbearers.

That was the plan anyway. But changes had to be made at the last minute to accommodate "an estimated 2,500 persons" who showed up in what was believed to be "one of the largest Amish funerals ever held in Ohio" and possibly the largest funeral ever in Holmes County.[33] Because the Coblentz barn could not hold that many people, an additional service was held on the front lawn and a third at the barn of Levi Weaver, less than half a mile away. The bonneted women sat on one side and the men on the other, occupying hard, backless benches.

The first sermon was delivered by Bishop Emanuel Schrock of Iowa, who had formerly been a member of the Mount Hope community. Bishop Jacob Mast was the first to speak at the services on the front lawn, while Bishop Henry J. Miller—the man who had presided over Paul's marriage to Dora—spoke first at Weaver's barn.

"If those two men could just be here now and see what sadness they have caused," Bishop Miller lamented.[34]

Because alcohol was thought to have figured in the crime, Bishop Fry took the opportunity to expound on the virtues of temperance. Another speaker praised the work of law enforcement and the benefits of living in a country where such criminals are brought to justice. As later recounted by Noah J.B. Miller, the sermons emphasized Paul's "true Christian character" as reflected in the way he always honored his parents and his refusal to "fight back at the bandits or protect himself with weapons"—his martyrdom.[35]

Although it was the custom for the coffin to rest on a bench in the barn during the service, this had to be abandoned due to the three separate services. Instead, it was kept in a small, carpet-less room in the Coblentz home until the services concluded. It was then moved to a spot beneath a pine tree on the front lawn, and the lid was removed. Two lines, men and women, filed past.

"It was a picturesque scene," Clair Stebbins wrote in the *Columbus Dispatch*. "The men in their dark suits, home-made white shirts and black felt hats; the women with white prayer-coverings on their heads. Last to view the body were the widow, still showing the effects of the attack three nights before, and other members of the family."[36]

Paul would have been dressed in a white shirt, white pants and a white vest, per Revelation 3:5: "He that overcometh, the same shall be clothed in white raiment." A woman would have been dressed in a white cape and apron—the same one she wore for her wedding and communion—and a white dress that has been reserved specifically for her funeral. These garments are generally made years in advance. One Amish woman purportedly washed, starched and ironed her own funeral attire every month so that it would be ready when needed.

Lunch followed, served in the house. "The people who don't go along to the graveyard start with lunch. Young ladies are on hand to serve coffee and

Paul Coblentz's modest headstone at Troyer Cemetery. *Author photo.*

refill water glasses," Rebecca Miller related. "The men and boys (helpers) eat, too, so they're ready to take care of the horses when the others return from the graveyard."[37]

Only about three hundred of the mourners made the trip to the cemetery, but that involved dozens of buggies and a few automobiles following the horse-drawn wagon bearing the coffin. The graveyard service ended at two o'clock, five hours after the funeral began. Despite their stoic appearance, the Amish experience grief, loss and sorrow the way all humans do. To quote Rebecca Miller: "We mourn not as those who have no hope."[38]

As the Amish struggled to come to terms with this tragedy that had been inflicted on their peaceful community and begin the healing process, the rest of the world would struggle to understand exactly who these oddly dressed people were. Abraham Hochstetler, who was raised Old Order Amish, recalled, "Grandfather always said that the incident was sad, but that Paul gave his life which saved his family, much like what the Savior did for all of us, so that portion of the event was to be celebrated."[39]

Chapter 2

MARTYRS MIRROR

The blood of the martyrs is the seed of the church.
—Tertullian[40]

I n 1897, the *St. Louis Globe-Democrat* reported on "A Peculiar Ohio Community":

> *There are no churches and no ministers in the community, which consists of 15,000 or 20,000 souls, residing on 160 acre farms. Every member of the settlement is a producer. Religious meetings are held, but they are at the homes of various members, not in regularly established meeting places....The customs of the people are primitive in their simplicity. No one ever thinks of knocking at a neighbor's door; they just walk in. Travelers who come through the community are taken in and entertained, in literal interpretation of the Scriptural injunction, and no one is permitted to receive pay for the entertainment.*[41]

This "peculiar" community was located in Holmes County. The Amish had been in Ohio since the early 1800s, settling mostly in the northeastern part of the state, but with pockets elsewhere. They were drawn by good farmland and religious freedom. They asked for nothing more than to be left alone to practice their faith—separated from the modern world. However, their distinctive manner of dress, speech (a variant of German) and system of beliefs have sometimes led to their being the targets of prejudice. But it once was much, much worse.

Old Order Amish still depend on horses for farming. *From the* Columbus Citizen-Journal, *Scripps-Howard Newspaper/Grandview Heights Public Library/Photohio.org.*

The Amish and the Mennonites were an offshoot of the Protestant Reformation, which swept through Europe in the sixteenth century. They were Anabaptists—rejecting infant baptism in deference to baptizing adult believers. This put them at odds with the Roman Catholics and the emerging Protestants denominations, which regarded them as heretics. Founded by Menno Simons, a former Roman Catholic priest from the Netherlands, the Mennonites were opposed to violence in any form, refused to participate in government and forbade marriage outside of their group.

Toward the end of the seventeenth century, a Swiss Mennonite named Jakob Ammann began to criticize his own church. He felt that it did not go far enough in withdrawing from the world in order to live in their own, more holy community, as the Bible commanded: "Come out from among them, and be ye separate, saith the Lord."[42] Soon, he was joined by a group of like-minded Mennonites in adopting a more primitive lifestyle. They would come to be known as Amish Mennonites, or simply Amish. And they, like other Anabaptists, would be persecuted for their beliefs.

Martyrs Mirror—or *The Bloody Theater*—is a book that once was second only to the Bible in Amish and Mennonite households. It remains popular to this day. First published in 1660, it is an encyclopedic account of more than four thousand Anabaptists who died rather than renounce their faith. While it is gruesome reading, these stories and testimonies serve as a reminder that Jesus never said the way would be easy. True believers might even find it comforting, knowing they are not alone in their suffering.

Dirk (or Durk) Willem is perhaps the most famous of the Anabaptist martyrs. Born in the Netherlands, he was baptized as a young man and thereafter rejected infant baptism in both word and deed. This brought him into conflict with the Roman Catholic Church, which had him imprisoned in a former palace. However, he subsequently escaped using a rope made out of rags. As he was fleeing across a frozen pond, one of the prison guards pursued him. But the guard was heavier than Dirk, who had lost weight while in prison, and broke through the ice. Bound by the tenets of his faith, Dirk returned to save his pursuer from drowning. He

Anabaptist Dirk Willems's inspiring death is chronicled in *Martyrs Mirror*. *Wikimedia Commons.*

was then recaptured, tried for heresy and burned at the stake on May 16, 1569—another martyr to his faith.

All thirteen American colonies originally had some form of state-supported religion. However, William Penn guaranteed religious freedom in Pennsylvania when he signed the Charter of Privileges in 1701. Himself a member of a persecuted group—the Quakers—Penn welcomed all faiths to his "Holy Experiment," and many Anabaptists, Lutherans, German Reformed and other groups began arriving soon thereafter, fleeing persecution in Europe. After the Northkill Creek watershed region in eastern Pennsylvania was opened for settlement in 1736, many Amish began arriving as well.

During the French and Indian War, Northkill, Berks County, was attacked by local Indians on September 19, 1757, under the direction of three French scouts. The house of Jacob Hochstetler, an Amish man, was set ablaze. When the Hochstetlers could no longer withstand the heat, they tried to escape out a window. "As they emerged, a young warrior, Tom Lions [or Lyons], about 18 years old, who had lingered behind gathering ripe peaches, observed them and gave the alarm."[43] Jacob's wife, Anna, along with a daughter and a son were slain, while Jacob and another son were taken captive.

Not long afterward, Lions moved to Ohio. He was living in a hut north of Berlin, Holmes County, when the Ammon brothers—Jacob and Henry—squatted on land near the Hardy settlement. Both men had been soldiers in the War of 1812. Jacob initially befriended Tom, but they subsequently had a falling out over a gun the Indian borrowed.

Later at a house raising in the Saltcreek settlement, the topic of the Hochstetler massacre came up. "Lions claimed to know much about it and justified the conduct of the Indians on that occasion," one historian recalled.[44] A relative of the Hochstetlers—it is not known whether he was Amish—overheard the Indian and said that he would "have satisfaction" for the murders. When Lions left the gathering that evening, he was followed by Jacob and the Hochstetler kinsman. He was never seen again and was presumed to have been murdered—possibly the first person murdered in Holmes County.

In 1809, Jonas Stutzman was the first white man to settle in eastern Holmes County. An Amish man born in Somerset County, Pennsylvania, in 1788, Jonas and his wife, Marie Magdalena Gerber, set up housekeeping along Sugar and Walnut Creeks. Three years later, David Hochstetler came to Walnut Creek Township, also from Pennsylvania. His nephew, Solomon Hochstetler, soon settled on an adjoining piece of property. Solomon had been widely suspected of murdering Susan, the young daughter of John Hochstetler, in Pennsylvania two years before. His accuser was a woman named Barbara Lehman.

Although the coroner's jury ruled that they did not know who committed the murder, the damage was done. As a family historian recorded, "Excepting his immediate family, nearly all [Solomon's] relatives believed him guilty…his brother could never be reconciled with him."[45]

When Solomon later sought to join the church, there was some reluctance to accept him. He finally convinced Bishop Moses Miller to baptize him, but only after he strenuously proclaimed his innocence of the murder. Even then, his brother, John, who had also moved to the area, would have nothing to do with them. Had Solomon confessed his guilt and repented, however, John would have been obligated to forgive him per his Amish faith.

Yet another Amish man had migrated from Pennsylvania to the same area. His name was Henry Yoder. Some fifty years after Susan's murder, Henry believed that he was dying and called a minister to his bedside. He confessed that that he had killed the girl. When word reached Solomon, he "wept like a child, and only wished John was living that he could go and see him and have a handshake."[46] As it turned out, Henry didn't die for several more years.

Soon the story emerged that Henry Yoder was "desperately in love with Barbara Lehman, which was not reciprocated, and he blamed John and his wife for alienating Barbara against him, in which he was not mistaken."[47] Then, on Sunday, March 4, 1810, he dropped by the house to see her. When he saw that Barbara and her sister were going to the sugar camp, he thought she was trying to avoid him. Angered, he killed the little girl in retribution.

Following Henry's confession, Bishop Levi Miller proclaimed a ban on him. He was to be shunned by all other members of the church community. The practice of shunning is derived from Matthew 18:15–17: "If your brother sins against you, go and show him his fault, just between the two of you.…But if he will not listen, take one or two others along.…If he refuses to listen to them, tell it to the church; and if he refuses to listen even to the church, treat him as you would a pagan or a tax collector."

Historically, shunning was one of the issues that led to the split between the Amish and the Mennonites. For many Amish, it is a very harsh punishment, especially for someone as old as Henry. However, Bishop Miller refused to relent, feeling that the offense was just too serious. But he told Henry that he would restore him if he first confessed his crime to a state court.

An Amish man drives a two-wheeled cart. *Cleveland Public Library/Photograph Collection.*

The two men subsequently went to Wooster, where they met with a Common Pleas judge, and Henry made a full statement. However, since the crime was committed in Pennsylvania, the case would have to be tried there. And half a century had passed. The girls' parents and nearly all of those who might have any testimony to give had died. The few who remained—Jacob Mast, Barbara Lehman and Solomon himself—would have had to travel to Pennsylvania to testify. Therefore, the matter was dropped, and the ban remained in place.

Throughout the nineteenth century, there were sporadic killings and suspicious deaths in Holmes County, but only one resulted in a murder conviction. That was the brutal slaying of Mary Mosenback (alternately Mosenbach or Mosenbaugh). In 1874, Henry Mosenback and his family had migrated to Walnut Creek Township from Baltimore, Maryland, where his first wife had passed away. He claimed to have met Mary "while she was a tramp on the road with two children. Her lineage was Irish, but she had a knowledge of German."[48] That was important because Henry did not speak English.

According to Henry, he agreed to marry her, but only if she disposed of the children. So she left them with others in Pennsylvania. Their subsequent marriage had been an agreeable one. However, sometime after a child was born to them, Henry began to suspect his wife of infidelity. She even left him for a few days and moved in with another man. Then, on February 13, 1876, Peter Ettling, a neighbor, called at their home. He sensed that there was tension between Henry and Mary but did not witness any violence.

After he left the Mosenback home, Peter stopped at the residence of Emanuel Beechey and shared his concerns. At about eleven o'clock, Emanuel decided to pay a visit to the Mosenbacks. Upon his arrival, he found the four-month-old baby on the floor crying and Mary dead nearby. He immediately hurried to Berlin to raise the alarm. A posse of men rushed to the house and concluded that Henry must have committed the deed after learning from Henry's seven-year-old son that he had fled to the woods.

Dividing into several parties, the men soon found Henry hiding behind a large beech tree. "He confessed to beating her with a round (rung) of a ladder," the *Holmes County Farmer* reported, although they found only an axe handle and a piece of a hay rick. "He did not intend to kill her, but 'supposed his violence caused her death.'"[49] He had also strangled her for good measure.

"A murder case in Holmes County was a novel thing. And there were rumors of some sentiment in the county for lynching Henry Mosenback. However, the *Holmes County Farmer* pronounced them untrue."[50] Henry pleaded guilty to second-degree murder and spent the next sixteen years in the Ohio Penitentiary.

What was trumpeted as the first murder trial in Holmes County in more than fifty years—since Henry Mosenback—took place in 1930. Maude Raynes, age thirty-four, was tried for slaying her common-law husband, John Sevastio, age forty-five, during a party at their home in Killbuck. She had originally "left her husband and three daughters in Waltonville, Pennsylvania, in 1925 to live with Sevastio."[51] Three years later, they relocated to Ohio.

Maude claimed that Sevastio often beat her and nearly drove her to suicide on two occasions. The shooting occurred after he had been drinking and started to attack her with a board. She killed him with a blast from a shotgun. However, the jury of ten men and two women acquitted her of his death.

Although Mossenback is a Germanic name, Henry was not Amish.[52] Neither were Maude Raynes nor John Sevastio. In fact, crimes committed by and against the Amish are rare—and rarely reported when they do occur. But they do occur, and in the summer of 1894, reports began to reach Toledo, Ohio, of "dastardly outrages" committed against the Amish settlement located several miles northwest of the city.[53] According to the *Columbus*

The Ohio Penitentiary was a hodgepodge of architectural styles. *Library of Congress.*

Dispatch, "Masked robbers forced an entrance to the house of a wealthy Amish German and secured four or five thousand dollars after torturing the man and his wife and brutally mistreating the grown daughters."[54]

The victim was believed to have recognized at least two of the men, but he refused to provide any assistance to law enforcement. This purportedly stemmed from the Amish belief that "under no circumstances, no matter how grievous the outrage, will they prosecute those who impose upon them. Even though the offense be murder, they will not lodge information, and they will go to jail rather than testify in court."[55]

A year later, the *New York Recorder* reported, "White Caps [vigilantes wearing white hoods] took a man named Henry Anker out into the woods…and, after tying him securely to a tree, flayed him nearly to death with withes."[56] The same week, "several masked marauders went to the home of an Amish family named Menkler and subjected them to all sorts of indignities, made them prepare a meal, after which they ransacked the premises, carried away valuables and insulted the aged mother and three young daughters grossly."[57]

During the same period, a party of men dressed as White Caps forced their way into the home of Joel William Handst, another Amish man. He had moved to Henry County from Pennsylvania a year earlier. "He would not associate with his neighbors, nor would he fight with any man including through the courts. Consequently, numerous depredations were made on his farm and no one was punished for it."[58]

Accused of being involved in the mysterious disappearance of several local farmers, Handst said nothing but "dropped to his knees in supplication while his tormenters inflicted all sorts of indignities upon himself and his family."[59] Finally, the men pushed him to the floor and cut his right ear entirely off and the left in half. But he also refused to cooperate with the sheriff, stating that he would leave the punishment of his attackers to God.

Knowing that they would escape punishment for their crimes, a handful of thugs had been routinely terrorizing the Amish who lived on farms scattered across Lucas, Henry, Fulton and Williams Counties—or so it was claimed. They had "destroyed their crops, crippled and tortured their livestock, and in some instances slaughtered sheep and hogs and taken the bodies away with them. Their wells have been befouled and their barns and outbuildings burned."[60]

One Henry County newspaper reported, "A species of warfare has been begun against [the Amish] by their enemies. Their buildings are burned, their crops destroyed and their cattle killed by lawless neighbors with the hope of driving them away."[61] However, there was also a counter-claim that reports of these alleged depredations were fraudulent and designed to keep Ohio governor William McKinley from campaigning for the presidency in other states.

What was clear from the newspaper accounts is that there was little understanding of who the Amish were and, more importantly, who they weren't. On June 21, 1911, authorities near Fredericksburg, Ohio, were looking into the tar and feathering of Michael Heilman by a band of masked White Caps the night before. Heilman had recently moved near a "peaceful" Amish settlement in Trail, and the initial suggestion was that "religious differences" may have been the reason for the assault.[62]

"Heilman appeared in Fredericksburg, the marshal said, wearing a heavy coat of tar and suffering seriously from the heat, but minus many feathers, as they were rather scarce at Trail, and he had managed to pluck himself fairly well before starting for Fredericksburg."[63] He had been removed from his home, stripped of his clothing, whipped and then coated with carbolic acid, red pepper and hot tar before being ridden out of town on a rail.

However, it was soon learned that Heilman, age twenty-eight, had been having an affair with Rebecca Volk, a married woman who was the mother of seven children, several of whom had been placed at the Wayne County Children's Home. They met when she came to Fredericksburg on a visit, and their conduct soon became a town scandal, especially after her husband learned of it and vowed revenge. When the woman subsequently moved to Trail, Heilman followed her, and they began living together as husband and wife.

Planning in secret, "twenty men and women, wearing white cloth masks, gathered about the house in which Heilman was staying. They carried with them several lengths of rope, a large bottle of carbolic acid, a quart of red pepper and a smoking bucket of tar, with plenty of feathers."[64] They surprised him while he was sitting in the living room of the house where he was staying. When the leader tapped on the window, Heilman looked up and saw a row of masked faces. He did not try to escape. Afterward, he walked fourteen miles before collapsing on the road. He purportedly lost the sight in his right eye.

Although this would have been a very un-Amish thing to do, some people, at least initially, tried to pin the assault on these "peaceful" but mysterious people. But there was no hint of Amish involvement.[65]

In October 1928, a twenty-eight-year-old man was arrested near Berlin, Ohio, for entering an Amish home after midnight in search of girls. Three or four members of the household restrained him and called Holmes County sheriff Chester Deringer. Two other men who were waiting outside in a car fled, but one was apprehended later. Then, in April 1936, Clarence Noland, age twenty-nine, of Amity, near Plain City, was committed to the Lima State Hospital for the Criminally Insane owing to an attack on two Amish sisters. He had cut them with a knife.

During July and August 1949, a gang of six young men had terrorized Tuscarawas and Holmes Counties, committing a number of armed robberies. Most of the victims were Amish, so it took a while for authorities to learn of the incidents. In the end, all six were sentenced to the Ohio State Reformatory in Mansfield for ten to twenty-five years.

In a series of four holdups carried out in November 1953, netting them a total of twenty-five dollars, two youths were found to be robbing Amish men who were out riding in their buggies. In each case, the young men swerved their car into the path of the buggy, forcing it to come to a halt. A black-haired youth, aged about twenty-two and wearing a red bandana across his face, held the driver up with either a shotgun or a rifle. Sheriff

An Amish family photographed by Cleveland's Jasper Wood. *Cleveland Public Library/ Photograph Collection.*

Deringer finally caught a break when one victim provided a description of the bandit. "The robber, whose light green 1950 Buick has been recognized in each case, stopped two buggies on the Mt. Hope–Winesburg road last night within 15 minutes but received only $18 loot."[66]

On the night of March 23, 1957, Lester Miller, age twenty, an Amish man, was beaten mercilessly in Holmesville, site of a series of such attacks. "The youth's parents brought him to Pomerene Memorial Hospital here May 1 in a 'convulsive and stuporous' condition. Dr. A.J. Earney said the youth appeared 'bewildered' but the diagnosis failed to uncover the reason."[67] He was transported to the Cleveland Clinic, where he underwent surgery. Although no charges were filed, Miller's parents claimed that he and two other Amish men were attacked by five Holmesville youths who beat him about the head. "Both youths told their parents that the attackers said, 'We've warned you Amish to stay out of Holmesville.'"[68]

Throughout their history, the Amish have encountered sporadic incidents of mistreatment by non-Amish. The term "claiping" or "claping" refers specifically to minor assaults committed against the Amish—such as throwing stones at their horses and buggies.[69] However, murder was something else entirely. It was a new chapter not only for the Amish in Ohio, but for Holmes County sheriff Harry Weiss as well.

Chapter 3

BIG-TIME SHERIFF

Bloodhounds ordinarily won't attack a person after tracking him down.
But just to be on the safe side we carry a little cooked liver to hand out as a reward.
—Sheriff Harry Weiss

The sheriff of Holmes County in 1957 was Harry Weiss (pronounced "Weese") and had been, off and on, for more than twenty-two years. A lifelong Democrat, Weiss was repeatedly reelected—six terms in all. In many respects, he was a remarkable man. At the time he took office, he had no special training or experience in law enforcement. He had previously spent ten years with the Ohio Fish and Game Department as a game warden—his duties included such things as having a man arrested for destroying a den of skunks. However, just six years later, he was being acclaimed as a "Big-Time Sheriff in Small Town"—and few would disagree.

A onetime pugilist, sometime musician, skilled marksman and father of seven, Weiss had taken "part in the Dillinger roundup, [had] aided state troopers in capturing escaped convicts, and [compiled] a record of 1185 arrests since Jan. 7, 1935."[70]

Harry Rudolph Weiss was born in 1898 to Leander Weiss and his wife, Dora Louise Leyman, in Walnut Creek Township, Holmes County. He was the second eldest of five children—two boys and three girls. His father was a farmer who lived his entire life—eighty-seven years—on the same Barrs Mills farm where he was born. Both parents were Swiss-German but spoke English. Not only would they one day experience the pride of having their son elected sheriff, but also the embarrassment of having him forced out of office a decade later. But many politicians can shed shame like a snake sheds its skin—and Harry was an adept politician too.

As the woman behind the man behind the badge, Harry's wife, Edith Mae Brand, was no less remarkable. It was a role she apparently relished. "On January 1, 1935, Edith Brand Weiss, husband Harry, their five sons and one daughter moved into the Holmes County jail in Millersburg, Ohio," according to *The Secret Life of a Lawman's Wife*, B.J. Alderman's chronicle of jailhouse families.[71] It was adjacent to the courthouse at 1 East Jackson Street. Darryl, Harry Jr., Billy, James Lawrence and Claire were the sons, and Evelyn Faye was the daughter. Another son, Richard, would be born there a year later. They would all play a part in what was, at the time, a "family business"—sheriffing.

In the primaries, Harry had been opposed by Errett Coessa Allison, a former deputy sheriff, and E.M. Cox, the current deputy. After his election, he would need a deputy, and one or the other of them was expected to get the job. After all, they both had experience—something he frankly lacked. He chose Allison.

The Weiss Family Orchestra, 1976: Harry Weiss Sr., caller; Marion Mackey, guitar; Darryl Weiss, saxophone; and Lola Moreland, accordion. *Middle*: Murray Gerber, piano; Mike Gerber, banjo; and Evelyn Weiss Gerber, banjo. *Amy Gerber Doerfler.*

Before taking office, Harry was best known for being the leader of the Harry Weiss Orchestra. "Members of the community as well as four of his seven children played in the band," music historian Amy Gerber Doerfler wrote. "The instrumentation included a fiddle, a trumpet, two saxophones, an accordion, a banjo, piano and drums."[72] And they played everywhere—high schools, grange halls, community festivals, armories—anywhere there was dancing.

When Harry decided to throw his hat in the ring, his band became his campaign committee. Harry's daughter, Evelyn, delighted in writing parodies of popular songs or composing jingles based on their campaign slogans. But everyone joined in. "On warm evenings, the family would pile themselves and their instruments into the back of a truck and drive around the county, singing their campaign songs."[73]

Burglaries, robberies, rustlings, accidents, shootings, sheriff sales, suicides, assaults, forgeries, "gypsies" (Romani) and various flimflams—they all fell within Harry's purview. He had barely moved into the jail when he announced that he intended to drive the bootleggers and slot machine operators out of the county. But when he wasn't occupied with rounding up bad guys—including Arden Kuhn (aka Arthur Sheffield), a bank robber and alleged associate of John Dillinger—he was assembling a small museum in the jail lobby. Among the various relics of pioneer days were old rifles and shotguns, arrowheads and hatchets, stuffed birds and animals.

Evelyn was a sophomore in high school when the jail became their new home. She recalled that after living "on a farm all their lives, it was quite a change to live in town and have all of the modern conveniences. What a heyday the children had, flushing toilets and turning the lights on and off! They'd hardly ever seen [an indoor] bathroom."[74] Just like on the farm, there were lots of chores to be shared in operating a jail and sheriff's office, and everyone was expected to pitch in. For example, they had to prepare and serve meals for the inmates.

One newspaper published a photo of Harry captioned "His Own Secretary." It said that both he and his deputy "must take care of all their reports, bookings, fingerprints, files, records, et al., without the assistance of a secretary."[75] However, he also was his own army. When he and his deputy went out on a call, they often armed themselves with a Thompson submachine gun. At times, they also packed sawed-off shotguns, tear gas bombs, guns, rifles, pistols and Billy clubs. Every once in a while, Harry would shoot a suspect with his riot gun or his submachine gun if they tried to flee.

The Holmes County Jail also served as the personal residence for the sheriff and his family. *Author photo.*

But with everything else that was going on, the family continued to perform in the parlor and for the public at community events. Harry played a homemade violin, while Edith played the piano. But not all of the band's members were family.

"Sheriff Weiss arrested a couple for forgery once and while they were incarcerated, it came to light that they, too, played instruments. So the forgers were added to the band and came along to the gigs and played their guitars."[76] The band also included a banjo player whenever he was arrested for drinking too much, which was often. Visitors sometimes found the sheriff in a jail cell jamming with the prisoners. "I haven't anything to do and these fellows aren't going any place," he once was quoted as saying.[77]

Harry was also something of a practical joker too. When Deputy Allison reported for work on the morning of February 16, 1937, he found the following notice on his desk: "Escaped from the Apple Creek institution for the feeble-minded, about 8:15 Monday evening, Man about 40 years of age, 5 feet 7½ inches in height, extremely long hair, very shabbily dressed, does not talk and will steal at every opportunity."[78] Allison was alone in the office, having been informed that the sheriff was out on a call.

Shortly thereafter, he received a call from Rottman's Drug Store in Millersburg that a mentally impaired man had been caught stealing merchandise. Suspecting it was the escapee, he rushed to the store and "found a mute, shabbily-dressed man who gesticulated his protest at arrest."[79] He forced the suspect to accompany him to the county jail, where he was found to have several hundred pennies in his pockets, a blackjack and a hair brush.

As several reporters looked on, Deputy Allison locked the "escaped lunatic" in a cell. He was about to notify Apple Creek that he had their man when several reporters asked to see the prisoner. Only then did he become suspicious. While newspaper accounts differ, either Allison removed the man's wig or Sheriff Weiss—for the prisoner was he—had slipped out of his disguise.

"I like a good joke and can take it," Allison purportedly said.[80] But he resigned three years later when his brother, Guy, announced that he would be running against Harry in the upcoming election.

In the course of his duties, Harry got to know the Amish in Holmes County fairly well. From a professional perspective, it was generally as the victim of some crime. For example, one of their carriages would be struck by an automobile. However, on rare occasions, they were the perpetrators. On May 15, 1942, Emmanuel L. Mast, age seventeen, shot his sister Sarah, twenty-one, in the face with a twelve-gauge shotgun. The family of nine was seated at the dinner table at the time. Sarah was taken to Pomerene Memorial Hospital in serious condition. Although Emmanuel readily admitted shooting her, he would not tell Sheriff Weiss why. Neither could Weiss learn any details from his parents, Mr. and Mrs. Leroy Mast of Mount Hope.

A decade after he first became sheriff, Harry had to investigate one of the worst tragedies in Holmes County history, not to mention his career. Three Amish youth died of carbon monoxide poisoning, and one narrowly escaped. On March 10, 1946, they were in a 1936 Ford (or Plymouth sedan) when they were overcome by fumes. The vehicle had become stuck in a mud hole, "just before the 'S' curve," on Country Road 235, three miles north of Mount Hope.[81] The dead youth were Levi Beachy, age fifteen; Aden Miller, eighteen; and Norman Mullet, seventeen. The only survivor was Emanuel "Manny" Schlabach, sixteen.

The Amish teens had left the Old Town Tavern in Winesburg in Mullet's car. A man had bought them beer. As Schlabach later recalled, "The roads at that time were neither blacktopped nor hard surfaced like they are nowadays, so there was an abundance of mud in the spring."[82] After the car got stuck in the mud hole, "we all agreed to sleep until morning and then

Sheriff Harry Weiss reviewing newspaper clippings. *From the* Columbus Citizen, *Scripps-Howard Newspaper/Grandview Heights Public Library/ Photohio.org.*

get somebody to pull us out."[83] But they did not realize that the exhaust pipe was buried in the mud.

The four young men were last seen leaving Mount Hope just before midnight on Saturday, May 9. It wasn't until Sunday afternoon that a passing motorist found them unconscious and near death. Others had passed by but assumed the four boys were sleeping. When Sheriff Weiss and his deputy, Harry Weiss Jr., were called to the scene, they found that bystanders had removed the three unconscious young men from the car. Beachy was already dead.

"The sheriff and deputy rushed the boys to Pomerene Memorial Hospital in Millersburg where oxygen was used to revive them," the *Coshocton News* reported.[84] However, only Schlabach recovered. One of the victims, Aden Miller, was a first cousin to Paul Coblentz. A fifth youth, John "Hans" Yoder, had been dropped off not far from his home just minutes before the tragedy occurred. His sister was Dora Yoder, Paul Coblentz's future wife.

The worst publicity Harry ever received—even worse than when *LIFE* magazine suggested he was a participant in the notorious 1944 Holmes County fox hunt—was when he was indicted by a grand jury on thirty-two counts of "unlawfully taking part of the salary of a woman deputy sheriff."[85] The woman was Frances Clos, and for thirty-two months he had "raked off" from $32.50 to $44.60 each month from her salary and kept it for himself.

Without explanation, Harry immediately repaid the money and resigned from office for "ill health" on July 1, 1946. Wayne D. Starner was appointed sheriff by the country commissioners, and that likely would have been the end of it. However, when Harry filed to run for the office in the November 5 election, the commissioners ordered the grand jury probe. Harry, who was forty-eight, was arraigned before Common Pleas judge Elmo Estill. After Harry pleaded guilty to the charges, Judge Estill fined him $320 and ruled that he must forfeit the sheriff's office should he get reelected.

After more than a decade as Holmes County sheriff, Harry was out a job—and a home. Eventually, he opened a shoe store. But Harry still had law enforcement in his blood. So, in 1952, he ran for sheriff once more, overwhelmingly defeating Starner in the Democratic primary. However, he lost to Chester Deringer. Four years later, he ran again, this time unseating Deringer after one term. Whether the voters had forgiven or forgotten his previous indiscretion, Sheriff Weiss was back in business, and all was right with the world. Clearly, the people liked their sheriff, flaws and all. This time, he would serve for four years, from 1957 to 1961.[86]

Jasper Wood took many candid photos of the Amish. *Cleveland Public Library/Photograph Collection.*

"This 'Mayberry-like' spirit was something that endeared the Holmes County public to the Weiss family," Doerfler wrote. "It also reflects what life was like in small-town America in the mid-1900s."[87] However, the sheriff of Mayberry, unlike Harry Weiss, never had to work a murder—and a murder in Amish country at that.

IN 1957, THERE WERE roughly six thousand Amish living in Holmes County, and Harry Weiss was their sheriff too. He was responsible for maintaining full police jurisdiction in all the county's municipalities, villages and townships. His command of German or Pennsylvania German was such that he was sometimes called on as an interpreter. For example, when Joseph J. Gingerich sued his wife, the former Mattie Miller, for divorce—a highly unusual occurrence among the Amish—Harry translated for him.[88] And on the night he was called to the Coblentz farm, Sheriff Weiss didn't have to be told where it was.

As Harry well knew, the Amish are far from being a homogeneous group. There are many subgroups within the faith, ranging from the ultraconservative to the relatively liberal. As they move toward the liberal end of the spectrum, they overlap with the Mennonites. A rule of thumb for separating the Amish from the Mennonites is their stance on buggies: the Amish use them, the Mennonites don't. Still, their religious beliefs are very similar.

John A. Hostetler, who was born Old Order Amish but later became a Mennonite, was the pioneer in the study of the Amish. Such later scholars as Donald B. Kraybill, Karen M. Johnson-Weiner and Steve M. Nolt have built on his work in identifying at least forty Amish "affiliations"—a term originally defined by Hostetler as "a group of church districts that fellowship together and share a common Ordnung."[89]

Ordnung is the German word for "order." It includes both written and unwritten guidelines for how the members of a particular church are expected to conduct themselves. No less an authority than "Lebanon" Levi Stoltzfus, erstwhile star of *Amish Mafia*, has noted, "Everything Amish traces back one way or the other to the Ordnung. Beards, marriage, divorce, shunning, pacifism, dressing plainly, avoiding modern technology—matters large and small, subtle and obvious, all reside in the Ordnung….Each local bishop gets to decide how the Ordnung applies to the issues of his congregation."[90]

True crime novelist Gregg Olsen noted:

The Ordnung isn't static; it can change and has changed, in some groups more than others….The Amish make a distinction between ownership and use. In the 1920s the Amish set rules concerning modern life that stand today: they may ride in a motor vehicle but not drive one, and they may use a telephone but not have one in the house. After all, no one would visit if they could phone instead.[91]

However, Christopher Petrovich, an independent scholar, believes that other researchers have gotten it wrong and has provided his own classification system.[92] While both camps likely have their points, Petrovich's model has the benefit of simplicity. An Amish convert, he asserted that many of the distinctions made by Kraybill and the rest are arbitrary. He proposed five characteristics of affiliation: 1) Church discipline, 2) Technology usage, 3) Theological beliefs, 4) Community practices and 5) Shared identity. Using these five dimensions, he identified six major affiliations, ranging from the most conservative to the least: 1) Swartzentruber, 2) Kenton, 3) Andy Weaver, 4) Old Order (mainstream), 5) New Order (traditional) and 6) New New Order.

Applying his "Traditional-Revised" model to Holmes and Wayne Counties in Ohio, Petrovich found that all six affiliations were represented, making Holmes-Wayne the most diverse of the country's five largest Amish settlements.[93]

The Coblenz family belonged to the Old Order Amish, which is the largest group both in Ohio and Pennsylvania. The image that comes to mind when most people think of the Amish is the Old Order. Although there may be local differences dictated by a particular *Ordnung*, they share some general characteristics.

In terms of doctrine, the Old Order Amish follow the Dutch Mennonite or Dordrecht Confession of Faith, which was originally adopted in 1623. Consisting of eighteen articles, it delineated such scriptural principles as a "belief in salvation through Jesus Christ, baptism, nonviolence (non-resistance), withdrawing from or shunning those who are excommunicated from the Church, feet washing ("a washing of the saints' feet"), and avoidance of taking oaths."[94]

However, the Old Order Amish split off from the Mennonites in 1693 over the failure of the Mennonites to enforce *Meidung* or shunning, as well as disagreement over foot-washing and the regulation of dress. They also believe that salvation can only be hoped for and is not guaranteed.

The Old Order Amish typically do not shun members who leave the church providing they join another Anabaptist church that practices

The Amish employ a variety of buggies, carriages and carts. *Library of Congress.*

separation from the world. As Johnson-Weiner has observed, "For the Amish, excommunication (*Bann*) and shunning (*Meidung*) are community-wide tough love."[95] The purpose of shunning is to help the former member of the congregation realize the error of his or her ways and repent.

The clothing worn by Old Order Amish is an expression of their faith and a connection with their history—an outward-facing symbol of belonging to the community and separation from the wider English world. It is distinctive and functional (often of polyester blend fabrics) and reinforces the virtue of humility. Women and girls wear modest dresses with long sleeves and full skirts, all of one color—often black, blue and white, although some groups allow purple, maroon, brown or gray. Younger girls might wear brighter colors as well, particularly in the summer.

Over the dress, they wear a cape and apron. They do not use buttons, but rather straight pins or snaps. Ideally, their dresses will be made from polyester and other synthetics that require the least amount of care, tend not to wrinkle and dry quickly on a clothesline—anything that makes the day-long task of laundry easier. The fabric must be heavy enough not to be sheer but light enough to be conducive to physical labor in the rural Ohio summer. Their stockings and shoes are black. Their hair is never cut, but rather worn in a braid or a bun on the back of the head and covered with a white prayer cap if married and a black one if single. And they never wear jewelry.

As for men and boys, they wear dark-colored suits with straight-cut, lapel-less coats, solid-colored shirts and broad fall trousers without pockets that button on the side and have a flap in the front. Although their shirts fasten with buttons, their suit coats and vests use hooks and eyes. Their shoes and socks are black. They are clean-shaven until they marry and then grow beards, but not mustaches. And their hats are black or straw, with the width of the brims and hatbands and the height of the crown determined by the *Ordnung*.

The Old Order Amish in Ohio are "house" Amish because they do not meet in churches, but rather in individual homes or even barns. A family typically hosts the service once a year. About 150 people might attend a regular three-hour Amish church service and the following fellowship meal, so preparation is important. Two weeks before a service, the women of the home will begin cleaning everything. That week, they will bake many loaves of bread, whoopie pies, cookies and other items with the help of their female neighbors. Church in a family's home is also the unofficial inspection day for said family. This is the day to show the bishops and neighbors what a good Amish family they are.

Only men are allowed to hold office in the church as bishops, ministers or other officials. And they do not seek the job. Women are permitted to vote in matters open to the whole congregation. The bishops, ministers and married men enter the church first, followed by the married women, who sit on the opposite side as their husbands, facing them. Next the unmarried women and girls, followed by the unmarried men and boys.

In 1919, Amish leaders decided that they should not connect to the electrical power grid, but it was not because they regarded electricity to be evil. They use flashlights, calculators and word processors that are battery powered. Similarly, they are not connected to gas lines but do use bottled gas for water heaters, stoves, refrigerators and lamps. Nowadays, many Amish carry cellphones, especially for conducting business.

The Holmes County Old Order Amish allow pickup balers, inside flush toilets, running water bathtubs, tractors for belt power, pneumatic tools, chainsaws, pressurized lamps and motorized washing machines. Sometimes they are permitted to use technology that they are not allowed to own. For example, the Amish may travel in cars, buses and trains, but not airplanes.

The Old Order Amish, according to Petrovich, "tend to see themselves within the narratives of the oldest communities."[96] They know the history of not only their faith but also their own families. Many Amish maintain extensive genealogies that can become quite complex as a result of the limited number of surnames due to a compressed gene pool. In Ohio, the most common ones are Miller, Yoder, Troyer, Raber and Hershberger. They also tend to repeat given names. Samuel, Jacob, John, Isaac, Abram and Mark are typical male names and Mary, Ruth, Martha, Sarah, Hannah and Miriam typical female names.

During the first half of the twentieth century, the Amish in Ohio clashed with the law on three main issues: evading the military draft, withholding their children from public schools and refusing to pay Social Security taxes. However, Sheriff Weiss does not appear to have been dragged into any of these constitutional quagmires. His relationship with the Amish was always a congenial one. He might be called on to investigate an occasional act of vandalism, possibly a missing child, maybe a robbery or, at worst, a buggy accident. But in nearly every instance, the Amish were the victims and not the perpetrators.[97] No doubt, they looked on Harry as a friend and trusted him to look out for their best interests. And by all accounts he did.

Chapter 4

KILLING TIME

He is a true fugitive who flies from reason.
—*Marcus Aurelius*[98]

An Amish farmer was dead—gunned down on a Thursday night as he tried to run from a couple of thugs who had forced their way into his home. And now they were the ones running. Running as they always did when they got into trouble. Running with no purpose except to escape. Running until they couldn't run anymore. Just running. By the time Sheriff Weiss organized a search in the vicinity of the Coblentz farm, the suspects had an hour's head start.

"Roadblocks were thrown up in the hopes of keeping the villains from escaping," Nathan Weaver recalled.[99] A ragtag posse of fifty to sixty men swarmed the gently rolling countryside. And bloodhounds were brought in from Portage and Columbiana Counties. But when the dogs could find no trace of the men in a nearby woods, the sheriff sent them away.

As Thursday bled into Friday, the as-yet-unidentified perpetrators somehow managed to slip through the dragnet that had been cast for them. "Neighbors, aware that the killers were still at large, waited until daybreak to venture into their barns to do their chores, for fear the men were lurking there," one historian later wrote.[100]

There was a brief flurry of activity when Mrs. Don Homan said she had seen two strangers on her farm near Fredericksburg. But the police found no sign of the men. For the moment, their trail had gone cold.

"The next morning," John Miller recalled, "a major breakthrough in the case came when a car was reported stolen in Fredericksburg, which is about 7 miles north of the crime scene. Missing was a 1953 gray and cream Pontiac four-door sedan with license number UY-704."[101] It belonged to Lloyd Crilow. At about three o'clock in the morning, the fugitives found the car with the keys in the ignition and a tank full of gas—at least that's what Sheriff Harry Weiss surmised.[102]

Word soon came that the stolen Pontiac had been spotted ninety miles away on State Route 80. According to the *Ohio State Journal*, "Mr. and Mrs. Forest Albright, who live several miles south of Alliance, reported they saw a cream and green car which the slayers are believed to have stolen."[103] And Hazel Becker, who operated a market in the same area, said she "she saw two young men walking into a field behind a barn."[104] Both the Ohio Highway Patrol and the Stark County sheriff responded. A dozen cars were dispatched to the area but turned up nothing.

Back in his office, Sheriff Weiss went to work attempting to identify the culprits. Dora remembered that one of the men—the shorter one—had

The abandoned truck stolen from the Holmesville lumberyard. *Holmes County Clerk of Courts.*

removed her gold-framed eyeglasses. By the time the glasses were located, "a report came in that a truck had been found stuck and abandoned in the ditch a few hundred yards south of the Coblentz farmstead by the Salt Creek Township House where CR 235 and SR 241 merge."[105] A half-hearted attempt had been made to set fire to the upholstery.

Weiss was quoted as saying that they had been able to lift good fingerprints from both Dora's glasses and the truck's steering wheel.

"We're hoping we can identify the men," Weiss said, but it would be a time-consuming process trying to tie them to anyone in the files.[106] Fortunately, Dora had been able to provide fairly good descriptions of both men. They seemed to match Chester Carter and Michael "Mike" Dumoulin. Two local boys, they had vanished shortly after the murder took place. A bulletin was broadcast to law enforcement agencies throughout the country.

Mike was from Wooster in adjoining Wayne County. He had a prior juvenile record and was "on parole from Ashland, Ky., Federal prison where he served a term for a Philadelphia auto theft."[107] Chester, from nearby Shreve, also in Wayne County, was slender and had dark, bushy hair. Both were age twenty and purportedly hung out together.

Then, on Saturday, July 20, Emery Baldwin, the constable of Lacon, a small town in central Illinois, was shot as he was making a routine check on a fishing cabin on the Illinois River, three and a half miles north of town. Stepping out of his boat, Baldwin was approaching the building when he was struck by rifle fire. A few rounds pierced his shoulder and back.

"A man soon rushed out of the cabin with a gun, followed by another man," according to one account. "The two rogues, one tall and dark, the other short and blond, ran to the water's edge and jumped into a boat [actually a kayak] and made their way down the Illinois River."[108] They had paused just long enough to shoot a hole in the bottom of Baldwin's outboard motor boat. Baldwin, age fifty, was lucky. There would be no kill-shot this time.

By eleven o'clock Saturday morning, a full-blown manhunt was underway. The discovery of the stolen car stashed in the woods across the road from the cabin linked them to the murder of Paul Coblentz. Led by Marshall County sheriff James A. "Jay" Evans, a posse of twenty police officers and a bloodhound beat the bushes along the river on Saturday night, looking for any sign of the men who assaulted the constable. Evans was thirty-three and a former marine who had seen combat in the South Pacific during World War II.

"A coast guard boat searched the river and its backwaters," Nathan Weaver recalled. "A highway patrol plane scoured the area from the air, but

From right to left: James Evans, Darrel Weiss, Harry Weiss and Ted Geib stand outside the suspects' hideout. *From the* Columbus Citizen, *Scripps-Howard Newspaper/Grandview Heights Public Library/Photohio.org.*

the search produced no villains. The search on Sunday was also fruitless."[109] They knew little about the men they were seeking except that one might be a suspect in the murder of an Ohio farmer. Evans theorized that they were headed downstream to Peoria.

Chester Carter soon surrendered—not to Sheriff Evans, but to Captain Glen Auckerman some 460 miles away in Wooster. On Saturday night, Chester was in Fredericksburg when he heard on the radio that he was a wanted man. Early the next morning, he was apprehended without incident in front of a diner after Dora tentatively identified the young man based on a mugshot.

According to the *Massillon Independent*, Carter "insisted that at the time Coblentz was shot he was nearby at his grandmother's home in Shreve, packing some clothes to leave town."[110] He said that he "had promised a judge he would leave town last week when he was fined $100 and given a 30-day jail sentence on a charge of intoxication and disorderly contact."[111] He was lodged in the Wayne County Jail, where Sheriff Weiss planned to question him using a polygraph. The suspect had a long history of alcohol abuse, which also involved assault and battery—but nothing approaching murder.

Nevertheless, newspapers reported that "FBI agents in Peoria, Ill., [had] identified both Carter and Dumoulin as possible suspects on the basis of fingerprints taken from a truck stolen from the Holmesville Lumber Co., shortly before the shooting."[112] Back in Ohio, though, Sheriff Weiss had his doubts and voiced regret over jumping the gun by naming Chester as a suspect. He wondered if the killers were still traveling together.

While Chester sat in jail, the hunt for the "baby-faced" Mike Dumoulin continued.[113] Sheriff Weiss reported that Illinois police officers believed they had him trapped in a swamp along the Illinois River. There was no town of consequence within fifty miles, and according to Weiss, "people in the area were on the lookout for the suspect and that they figure he will have to leave the swamp for food or water soon."[114]

More than sixty years later, Mike related that there were many islands in the river. They tied up at one and hid there all day and all night. Camouflaged by the branches of the willow trees, they watched the officers searching for them before finally abandoning their kayak.

Other details regarding the murder suspects began to emerge, and a timeline was pieced together. "After attending a homecoming on Wednesday night," Nathan Weaver later recalled, "the two buddies went groundhog hunting after the local man got off work at 4:30 on Thursday evening. Two fellow hunters picked them up and dropped them off at the Holmesville Inn around 7:00 P.M."[115]

Built as a bank nearly fifty years earlier, the Holmesville Inn occupied a small building constructed of rock-face concrete block on the corner of West Main Street and North Millersburg. The business was eventually forced to relocate to the edge of town due to ongoing complaints about the tavern's proximity to a school just a block away.

Jerry Knapp, owner of the bar, told a highway patrolman that two men matching the suspects' descriptions came into his tavern at a quarter past seven on Thursday evening and ordered cheeseburgers and pitchers of beer.[116] They were bare-headed and wore overalls and shirts. One man had a hunting license pinned to his belt in back. He also had a rifle. The shorter of the two had blond hair, and the taller one had dark hair and long sideburns and was slim.

Atlee Mullet of Berlin reported having seen two men in the cab of a ditched flatbed truck at 10:15 p.m. Thursday, about half an hour before the

Main Street Pizza now occupies the former Holmesville Inn. *Author photo.*

murder. The driver had a skinny face and sideburns to the ear lobes. Mullet was owner of the Mullet Coal Company.

"On Monday the 22nd, at 5:00 A.M.," John Miller wrote, "a Studebaker pickup truck was reported missing from a farm near Henry, Illinois, six miles north of Lacon. It was widely suspected that the truck was stolen by the fugitives, so yet another roadblock and search were conducted in that area."[117] When it ran out of gas, however, they ditched it just north of Toulon.

Elmer Hampton, a local high school teacher who was on his way to work, gave the two men a ride to where State Route 91 intersected with State Route 34. From there, they walked south to where 34 turns west to the town of Galva.

Not long afterward, Don Blakey, a milk hauler for Kraft Foods, tipped off police that two men were seated on a concrete abutment at the Indian Creek "Y." He thought they matched the descriptions of the fugitives. Stark County sheriff Burt W. Eltzroth immediately responded. Arriving at the intersection—the Galva "Y"—he found "the two young men were still there, waving their thumbs in the air, hoping desperately for a new ride and a new chase, but none came."[118]

Assisted by Marshal Theodore R. Knowles and trooper Rollin "Buzz" Pugh, Eltzroth arrested the fugitives at gunpoint at 8:05 a.m. No longer

Clockwise from left: Mike Dumoulin, Sheriff James Evans and Gene Peters. *Holmes County Clerk of Courts.*

armed, they offered no resistance. They admitted to being Michael "Mike" Dumoulin, age twenty, and Cleo "Gene" Peters, nineteen. Their arrest brought an end to a four-day manhunt and seemed to clear Chester Carter. Years later, Dumoulin denied knowing anyone by that name.

"Officers who captured the pair said Dumoulin accused Peters of shooting the Lacon constable," according to the *Marion Star*. Sheriff Evans said that Dora's descriptions tallied with the two men. Constable Emery Baldwin "also identified Peters as the man who shot him."[119] Gene said he was "scared" when he did it. Years later, Mike claimed, "After [Gene] shot that constable, I busted those rifles up. I just wanted to make sure that he didn't shoot nobody else."[120] Although the guns were tossed in the Illinois River, a search was soon underway to locate them.

On Tuesday, July 23, Sheriff Weiss, along with his son Darryl and Ted Geib—both deputized for the trip—traveled to Lacon to pick up the two suspects.[121] He had a few murder warrants in hand. Even as they were en route, a report surfaced that John Hershberger, an Amish farmer living near the village of Charm, had taken his eleven-year-old son, Andrew, to Pomerene Hospital in Millersburg.

Andrew claimed that he was shot while near a woods not far from his home. He had sustained "flesh wounds under his left arm, on his face and his right hand."[122] Right away, people began trying to connect this shooting with the murder of Paul Coblentz. However, Andrew's story soon fell apart. He admitted that he and his brother, Monroe, had found a dynamite cap on a ledge in a buggy shed. They detonated it by placing a chisel on top of the cap and striking it with a hammer.

Sheriff Weiss revealed that Mike and Gene were questioned for more than four hours on Tuesday evening at the Marshall County Jail. The suspects purportedly admitted that they were in the Coblentz home when the Amish farmer was killed. In addition, the missing rifle was recovered in the Illinois River swamp and turned over to Weiss. It was a .25-20 lever-action Marlin that George Dumoulin said his son had left the house with on Thursday.

Waiving extradition, Mike and Gene agreed to return to Ohio with Sheriff Weiss on Wednesday, July 24. County Prosecutor James Estill announced that the two men would be held at the Holmes County Jail without bail. He had yet to decide whether to call for a special grand jury or wait until the regular one convened in September.

Weiss had originally identified Mike as a suspect after an unidentified "woman who had been out with Dumoulin and his friend told the sheriff she felt they may have been the murderers."[123] Presumably this was in Shreve. Mike had an arrest record going back to when he was twelve. It included two charges of breaking and entering, petit larceny and being AWOL from the navy. However, Gene was unknown to local law enforcement. Then there was Carter. Admittedly, he resembled Gene. Even after he was cleared of any involvement in the murder, he was kept in jail to serve out a $100 fine for disorderly conduct and intoxication levied by Mayor Lew Crawford of Shreve.

The two suspects arrived back in Millersburg in shackles via a police escort at about three o'clock in the afternoon. Darryl Weiss drove the stolen getaway car. Per the *Daily Times*, "Prosecutor [James] Estill and Sheriff Weiss, who found a crowd of about 50 waiting when they arrived here, hustled the two prisoners into the sheriff's living quarters and then placed them in cells."[124] This enabled them to bypass the main entrance to the jail and avoid those who were waiting to have a look. Estill refused to allow press photographers to take pictures or reporters to speak with the prisoners. "We will not permit them to be unduly subjected to publicity until after we have held a preliminary hearing," he asserted.[125]

When booked into the Holmes County Jail, Cleo Eugene Peters was listed as six feet, three inches tall and 175 pounds, with brown hair and blue eyes. He was nineteen years old, having been born on March 29, 1938, in Muscatine, Iowa. He attended school in Eliza Township, Mercer County, Illinois. Michael George Dumoulin was five feet, seven inches tall and 134 pounds, with brown hair and blue eyes. He was twenty years old, having been born in Millersburg on December 19, 1936. However, he grew up in Wooster.

Mike had previously been arrested on June 1, 1955. At the time, he was AWOL from the USS *Iowa* (BB-61), a battleship docked in Philadelphia. He was also charged with petit larceny. Nine days later, he was released to the navy, which led to his imprisonment at the Federal Correctional Institution (FCI) at Ashland, Kentucky. That was where Mike met Gene.

Opened in 1940, FCI is a low-security institution operated by the Federal Bureau of Prisons. It was "primarily designed to house short-term offenders of the non-habitual type."[126] Most inmates were between the ages of fifteen and twenty-two years. They performed all of the repair work in the prison, operated a 250-acre farm and even attended classes at a nearby college. According to a newspaper article, "This new concept of treating young lawbreakers is a result of the 1950 Federal Youth Corrections Act."[127]

Prior to Gene and Mike's commitments, the institution had held some famous inmates, including four of the "Hollywood Ten"—John Howard Lawson, Albert Maltz, Adrian Scott and Dalton Trumbo. Along with Dashiell Hammett, they were all writers charged with contempt of Congress because they would not cooperate with the House Committee on Un-American Activities investigation into communist activity in the United States.

On Thursday, July 25, Gene and Mike found themselves sitting in the Holmes County Jail, awaiting a preliminary hearing. Mike occupied a cell on the first floor, while Gene was confined in one on the second. Shortly after he was booked, Mike had met with attorney Marion F. Graven. Gene, however, had yet to be assigned counsel. Sheriff Weiss and Prosecutor Estill had conferred that morning before releasing a press release in the afternoon. "We still have a lot of work to do on the case before we will ask for the hearing," Estill told the press. "There are many facts to be checked."[128]

With or without legal representation, the two suspects continued to disclose details concerning the night of the murder. They had become friends at FCI in Kentucky. Gene had quit school at seventeen—("after the eighth grade")—to join the U.S. Air Force.[129] During basic training, he went AWOL and stole a pickup truck in Muscatine in order to drive to Tennessee "to see a girl I knew."[130] As a result, he was sentenced to prison for driving a stolen vehicle across state lines.

Gene was released in January 1957. Mike got out in June. On July 16, 1957, Gene received a letter from Mike inviting him to visit Wooster "to blow off steam and have a good time."[131] Leaving that same day, he hitchhiked to his friend's house, arriving at 4:30 p.m. The two men decided to go hunting, but at some point they abandoned that idea and went drinking at the Holmesville Inn instead. After consuming a few cheeseburgers each and a couple pitchers of beer, they stole a truck from the R.J. Patterson Lumber Company in Holmesville.[132]

Reasoning that the truck would be reported stolen, they purportedly hatched a plan to shoot Sheriff Harry Weiss. "They were out to make headlines," Weiss related. "Dumoulin told me they had hoped to shoot me because a sheriff would make a bigger headline."[133] They knocked the rear window out of the back of the truck so they could fire their rifle out of it.

"They said they hoped I would get a report on the stolen truck and follow them," Weiss said. "I don't think they would have shot too accurately from a bouncing truck, though."[134] However, before any officers were alerted, the truck slid off a curve and into a ditch.

Years later, Mike said that he didn't even know Sheriff Weiss at the time—Starner was sheriff when he was previously arrested—and that the plan was simply to shoot out the tires of any vehicle pursuing them. They were drawn to the Coblentz home because "it was the only place near that had a light on."[135]

At a preliminary hearing on Friday, July 26, Gene, who was accused of the actual shooting, pleaded guilty to first-degree murder, while Mike pleaded innocent. It was anticipated that they would ask for separate trials. Although he believed they were "prepared to shoot it out with anyone who tried to stop them after they stole a truck in Holmesville," Weiss did not think they were "out to kill anybody the night Coblentz was slain."[136] In the same breath, though, he also dismissed them as "thrill killers."[137]

An "alienist" (i.e., psychiatrist) conducted group sessions at Lima State Hospital. *Authors' collection.*

Nearly a month later, on August 21, eighteen names were drawn from the jury wheel to make up the grand jury that would go into session on September 3. The jurors would consider indictments on all of the criminal cases that had been accumulating since the previous jury was convened in the spring. To no one's surprise, they returned indictments against both men. Mike and Gene were then arraigned before Judge Wayne W. Badger on the afternoon of September 9. Appearing in court separately, each was handcuffed to Sheriff Weiss. There were an estimated fifty spectators, about one-third of whom were Amish.

Both men pleaded not guilty and not guilty by reason of insanity to the grand jury indictments. Judge Badger ordered them transported to the Lima State Hospital for the Criminally Insane on September 16, 1957. Following a month-long observation and evaluation, officials at the hospital concluded that the men could stand trial.

"Identical reports from Henry Luedens, M.D., superintendent of the Lima Hospital, said after intensive observation and examination it was the hospital staff's opinion that Peters and Dumoulin are of average intelligence and are considered sane."[138] A psychiatrist, Luedens had previously been chief of staff at the Veterans Administration Hospital in Chillicothe. The suspects were then returned to the Holmes County Jail on October 18, 1957.

In a month and a half, the first trial would begin.

Chapter 5

TERROR AT THE AMISH FARMHOUSE

Two Killers Invade a Peaceful Ohio Colony.
—True Detective

Holmes County's first murder trial in a quarter of a century got underway on Monday, December 2, 1957, at the courthouse in Millersburg. Gene Peters, the alleged triggerman, would be tried first. His accomplice, Mike Dumoulin, would go on trial a month later. Each was charged with first-degree murder. If convicted, they could face the death penalty. Anyone hoping for a Perry Mason moment, however, would be disappointed.

Just a month before, *True Detective* magazine published an article about the Coblentz murder. Written by Hal White, "Terror at the Amish Farmhouse" was a muddle of fact and fiction. Not only did White occasionally confuse Mike with Gene, he included some imaginary dialogue ("Without the glasses you'd be a pretty dish") that harkened back to his pulp-fiction roots.[139] County prosecutor James Estill told a reporter for the *Holmes County Farmer-Hub* that he had refused to cooperate with a writer "who was trying to pick up a few extra bucks by compiling this tale for one of the blood-and-thunder detective magazines."[140] Perhaps he was referring to White.

Situated at the corner of East Jackson and South Monroe Streets, the three-story courthouse was completed in 1886. Designed by architect Joseph W. Yost, it had been built by local labor with locally quarried stone and locally fabricated metal. A statue of Lady Justice adorned the northern pediment, while a large clock crowned the center tower. No one could fail to

In November 1957, *True Detective* ran an article on the Coblentz murder. *Authors' collection.*

have been impressed, although some taxpayers balked at the cost, especially when the county commissioners had to borrow an additional $30,000 to complete the project.

On the west lawn of the courthouse was a limestone statue of a Union soldier atop a granite monument. On the east was a stone watering trough,

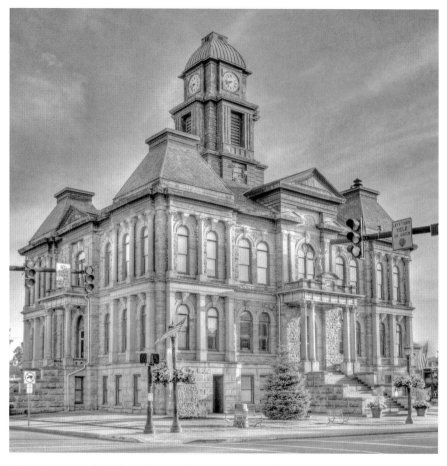

Millersburg's stately Holmes County Courthouse was built in the Italianate architectural style. *Alvintrusty, Wikimedia Commons.*

an iron hitching rail and a row of parking meters with a few signs reading "Horses Only." A rectangular jail of red brick built in the Italianate style in about 1880 squatted on the southwest edge of the grounds. Once again, it was occupied by Sheriff Harry Weiss.

The trial would take place in the third-floor Common Pleas courtroom, an ornate chamber with a Rococo ceiling. "The courtroom itself is of semi-classic design," Clair Stebbins of the *Columbus Dispatch* wrote. "The walls are green, broken by flat double-columns, beige in color. Sunlight filters through tan shades at the windows along the south side."[141] An American flag hung on the wall behind the judge's bench, along with two neatly framed photographs—one of W.S. Hanna and the other of William

Amish buggies tied up at a hitching rail outside the courthouse. *From the* Columbus Citizen-Journal, *Scripps-Howard Newspaper/Grandview Heights Public Library/Photohio.org.*

The beautiful Holmes County courtroom impressed reporters who attended the trial. *Author photo.*

N. Crow, the first two Common Pleas judges in Holmes County history. On the back wall was a similarly framed photograph of the third judge, Robert B. Putnam.

When court was called to session that morning, Judge William Wayne Badger was presiding. At age fifty-nine, Judge Badger was the fifth Common Pleas judge in the history of Holmes County. No picture was necessary since the man himself was regularly on view in the courtroom. The son of a local animal doctor, he was born in 1898 in Holmes County and graduated from the Ohio State University College of Law. He had been the prosecutor in the Maude Raynes case twenty-seven years before.

Early in 1956, Badger had participated in another murder trial. He was a member of a three-judge panel that convicted Earl Sullivan of Utica, Licking County, of killing his estranged wife, Valeria. She was in the process of suing her husband for divorce when he shot and killed her at the local American Legion Hall. Sentenced to death, Sullivan won a last-minute commutation by Governor Frank J. Lausche.

"I concluded that based upon the facts and circumstances in the case," Lausche said after studying the matter for ten days, "in my opinion my intervention is warranted."[142] This might have been taken as a good omen by the defense were it not for the fact that Lausche then resigned to become a U.S. senator and C. William O'Neill was now governor.

Just before leaving office in January, Lausche had commuted several first-degree murder sentences. The interim governor, John W. Brown, commuted five more. He also made a point of criticizing his predecessor for ignoring "more than 40 cases" that had then fallen to him.[143] At the time, only the governor could commute a sentence. Unable to review them all during his eleven days in office, Brown recommended that the law be changed to authorize the Pardon and Parole Commission to commute sentences subject to the governor's approval. So far, Governor O'Neill had permitted one execution to take place.

The prosecutor was James H. Estill. Born in 1927, he graduated from Ohio State in 1952 and was elected prosecuting attorney five years afterward. Handling his first criminal case ever, let alone murder case, he said that he would ask for the death penalty for the nineteen-year-old Iowa youth. James suspected that he would have difficulty obtaining a conviction because the Amish "are a forgiving people with deep religious convictions against capital punishment or even revenge."[144]

Assisting James was his father, Elmo M. Estill. Elmo had preceded Badger as the fourth Common Pleas judge in the history of Holmes County. As yet, no photograph of him hung on the wall either. Elmo was born in 1898 and had served as a private in a field hospital during World War I.

"As the county prosecutor in 1932, [Elmo Estill] secured the conviction of the last two men ever to be tried for murder here," the *Columbus Dispatch* reported.[145] Herbert Meeker and Ford Parker were both charged with killing their wives. Meeker, who brained his wife with an automobile pump, tried to pin the murder on a distant relative who had turned a shotgun on himself as the police were closing in. However, he copped to helping dispose of the body after driving over it with the car. In 1933, Meeker would pay the ultimate price in the electric chair.

Parker was accused of slaying his wife on June 29, 1932. Testimony established that he "shot his wife because she refused to return to his home in Applecreek with him."[146] Future judge Wayne Badger served as Parker's defense counsel, along with Bowers and Bowers of New Philadelphia. They attempted to show that "he was temporarily insane at the time of the shooting."[147] Judge Robert B. Putnam committed Parker to Lima State Hospital for observation.

Thirty days later, Parker was returned to Holmes County, having been pronounced "sane." But Putnam sent him back for another thirty after learning the hospital had been understaffed. Once again, Parker was pronounced sane and fit to be tried.[148] Although convicted of murder and sentenced to prison, "alienists at Ohio Penitentiary...demanded that [Parker] be saved from the electric chair and instead committed to the Lima State Hospital"—which he was.[149]

While serving as Common Pleas judge, Elmo Estill had presided over the trial of "one of the most dastardly crimes in the annals of Holmes County"—at least in the opinion of Probate Court judge Frank W. Fankhauser.[150] On October 15, 1948, four men had gang-raped an Amish woman at her home while her three children slept in an adjoining room.

That evening, the men went to the victim's house and attempted to lure her husband, Sam Miller, away by telling him that he was wanted at his place of employment. "Failing in this they commanded him to come out into the yard. While two of the intruders held him, each of the four men criminally attacked his wife," according to seventeen-year-old Harry M. Ober Jr., the youngest of the men and the admitted ringleader.[151] There were clear similarities to the Coblentz case.

As his father sat in Fankhauser's courtroom (his mother was deceased), Ober "confessed his part in the criminal act and was sentenced to three years in the State Reformatory at Mansfield."[152] It was said that only his youth had saved him from a life sentence. His accomplices—Mahlon Hostetler, age thirty-two, of Fredericksburg; Gene Weber, age twenty-one, of Cambridge; and John E. Duncan, of Fredericksburg, who turned eighteen on September 3, a month before the crime—were tried later for breaking and entering into the home for the purpose of committing a felony and criminal assault. Judge Estill sentenced each of them to the Ohio Penitentiary for three to twenty years. One of the rapists—likely Hostetler—was said to be Amish.

Although the Amish prefer not to engage with the court system, it would be wrong to think that they didn't care what became of Paul Coblentz's killer. While they customarily did not report instances of "claping" and even assault, they recognized that there was a need to draw the line when it came to serious injury or death.

So the Amish will testify in court when called on to do so. They may also attend a trial as spectators to observe justice in action. They will perhaps even use the event as an object lesson for their children—a real-life example of the wages of sin. But they were also interested in the fate of the killer. Not so much his sentence—although there was that too—but what would become of his soul. They would pray for him in the hope that he might receive God's forgiveness.

But what the Amish won't do is serve on juries, especially if it is a capital offense. They are opposed to the death penalty and generally avoid situations in which they are required to sit in judgment of others. It is part and parcel of the principle of nonresistance—of pacifism in the face of any and all aggression—that undergirds their daily lives. By law, however, they still had to be considered for jury duty.

Owing to the high interest in the trial, Judge Badger arranged for the press table to be set up just outside the railing ("the bar") in the courtroom. While he would not permit the taking of photos while court was in session, he was not opposed to them being taken before or afterward. Although the Amish generally declined to pose for them, many photographs were taken of them anyway.

Having been declared indigent, both Gene and Mike would be represented by public defenders. Gene was represented by Raymond O. Morgan and William F. Anfang Jr. and Mike by Marion F. Graven and William H.H. Wertz.

Born in 1906, Morgan was a graduate of Ohio State University; he served as prosecuting attorney in Wayne County for a number of years before entering private practice. He had handled a variety of cases, from a mother smothering her baby to sizable lawsuits. A resident of Orville, he was also active in Democratic politics.

Julius Fortis often captured visual irony in his photographs. *Mary Lou Kunkler.*

Anfang, Morgan's co-counsel, was born in 1920, presumably in Pennsylvania. A Roman Catholic, he served in World War II, belonged to the Knights of Columbus and lived on a farm called Pumpkin Hill outside Wooster.

The first order of business on Monday, December 2, was jury selection. An estimated one-fourth of the 110 men and women in the jury pool were Amish. As the lead attorney, Morgan attempted to use the Amish position on capital punishment for the benefit of their client, hoping to sway other prospective jurors. However, Judge Badger soon put an end to it by excusing the Amish, but only after they stated their opposition to the death penalty. There was no automatic exemption.

Morgan also repeatedly asked the jurors if they would be prejudiced by the introduction of evidence pertaining to the use of alcohol by the defendant. At one point, he referred to Peters as "a boy too young to vote."[153] However, Elmo Estill countered by pointing out that under the law "anyone who is 14 years of age is completely responsible for crime."[154]

By noon, twelve prospective jurors had been questioned and two were seated. At the end of the day, Gene was escorted out of the courtroom by Sheriff Weiss. On the way, he passed by his parents, Myron and Estella Peters, in the corridor. They had driven all the way from Muscatine, Iowa, accompanied by an aunt and uncle, Mr. and Mrs. W.T. Tapscott of Molline, Illinois. Myron was a factory worker, while Estella was a homemaker, caring for their four children. Because they had left the children at home—two girls and two boys ranging in age from six to seventeen—they were uncertain how long they could stay.

Nevertheless, they were said to be the two most attentive spectators in the courtroom, which was so jammed with people that they had trouble finding seats. Myron remained expressionless, staring straight ahead while the prospective jurors were examined. Estella, weeping softly much of the time, occasionally cupped her head in her hand. When a recess was called, she would try to get a word with her son, who sat on the other side of the railing. Once, she even grasped his hand briefly.

"Yes, he's been in trouble before—but not bad trouble," Myron told Stebbins. "Just the sort of thing that might happen to anyone."[155] He believed that his son's behavior was due to excess drinking. "He overstepped his limit," he said. "The boy was never denied a drink at home, but a can of beer was about his limit. This was something he was unaccustomed to."[156] The father argued that the crime wasn't premeditated, but rather the result of impaired judgment.

Mike's parents—George Joseph Dumoulin and Emma May Geiogue Dumoulin—also were on hand. The fate of their son was inextricably connected to that of Peters—a young man they had never met. Because Gene had been the gunman, they had reason to hope that their son would get off with a lesser sentence.

Since the night of the murder, many lives had been changed—some irreparably. Dora, Paul's widow, had taken their daughter, Esther, and moved back in with her parents. "For a long time," newspapers noted, "Esther was afraid upon hearing a dog bark."[157] She and her mother would not return to the house where the unthinkable had occurred.

Mose Coblentz, Paul's father, along with his wife and daughters, had also relocated. "The father has sold his farm equipment and personal belongings and has moved to the vicinity of Sarasota, Fla., where there is an Amish settlement. The farm near Mount Hope was too large for him to operate without help, he explained to friends."[158]

Jury selection resumed on Tuesday, December 3. "Five men and four women were tentatively seated in the jury box late this morning after 41 venire men [i.e., prospective jurors] had been examined," Clair Stebbins reported.[159] They were housewives, farmers, a hardware clerk, a baker and a worker in a lumberyard.

Based in Zanesville, Ohio, Stebbins was managing editor of the *Zanesville Times-Signal* before joining the *Columbus Dispatch* as a staff writer. Specializing in aviation, he had flown with Amelia Earhart and "splashed a little-known local Marine pilot by the name of John Glenn across the front page during the Korean War."[160] He also had a front seat to the launch of the first American into space. He would follow Coblentz murder from beginning to end.

Judge Badger appeared to be growing more impatient by the minute at how long the selection process was taking. Of the forty-one examined, thirty-two were excused for cause, including eleven Amish. Three more regular jurors and one alternate remained to be selected. The seated jurors couldn't get too comfortable though. As one newspaper noted, "Before the jury can be impaneled, however, County Prosecutor James Estill and Defense Attorney Raymond Morgan are each entitled to six peremptory challenges with which they may unseat jurors without giving a cause."[161]

"Of the 21 non-Amish excused from jury duty, 8 said they were opposed to capital punishment," Stebbins wrote, "7 said they had already formed an opinion, 3 submitted a doctor's certificate and another acknowledged she was a second cousin to attorney Elmo Estill of the prosecution."[162] One member of the prospective pool was unavailable because he had died, while another was in Switzerland on a trip. In addition to the original venire of seventy, another forty names had been added to allow for the Amish, who were expected to be excused.

Throughout the proceeding, Gene sat solemnly in the courtroom, restrained by handcuffs. Stebbins noted, with approval, "Young Peters has abandoned the shaggy Elvis Presley–type haircut with long sideburns that gave him a somewhat sinister appearance at the time of his arrest a few days following the crime. His hair is newly cut in normal fashion, he wears blue trousers, gray coat and well-shined black shoes. His shirt is open at the throat."[163]

As anxious as Judge Badger had been to get the trial underway, there was a delay due to a power failure that left the courtroom without lights. So he was forced to call an early recess for lunch. Then, when he seemed determined to keep the court in session beyond the regular time for adjournment, it began snowing so heavily that he had no choice but to dismiss everyone for the day. Before doing so, he advised them to be "prepared to go out into the weather" when they returned on Wednesday because they would be visiting the crime scene.[164]

The following day, Wednesday, December 4, the *Columbus Dispatch* ran a photograph showing Tobias Yoder, an Amish farmer, registering for jury duty. He would not be needed. Jury selection was completed that day. Consisting of six men and six women and one male alternate, the jury was culled from a jury pool of more than sixty people, twenty of whom were Amish. All of the Amish were excused because of their opposition to capital punishment.

Gene's parents had returned home to Muscatine, Iowa, the night before, but told attorney Morgan that they would be back before the trial concluded. For now, they had to tend to their other children.

In his opening statement, James Estill stated that he would be seeking the death penalty for Cleo Eugene Peters on the grounds that the murder was deliberate and premeditated. He planned to use the defendants' own words against them, having written statements from both of them, sixty-four pages in all, signed after their arrests.

However, attorney William Anfang insisted, "It was simply a case of a boy away from home, drinking with a companion. As a result this terrible tragedy came about."[165] There was, he declared, "No malice; no hatred. There was no revenge; no premeditations, thus, no motive."[166] He concluded by telling the jury, "The fate of the boy is in your hands—whether the boy lives or dies."[167]

Following lunch recess, the jury was scheduled to visit the crime scene. Judge Badger asked for volunteers to drive, but only those who had snow tires on their vehicles. They would be reimbursed for their expenses. The jury was then loaded into several cars and driven fifteen miles outside of Millersburg to the murder scene. While there, they tramped through the snow to see where Coblentz fell outside the door of the basement house. In addition, they spent about ten minutes inside the sparsely furnished and now unoccupied dwelling. Peters accompanied them, constantly puffing on a cigarette. He showed no obvious emotion but did not remain in the house more than a few minutes.

Before they returned to Millersburg, the jurors also saw the ditch a quarter of a mile away along SR 241 where the two men purportedly wrecked the stolen truck. Back in the courthouse, they would be tasked with conjuring up this cold, stark landscape as the attorneys and witnesses described the sequence of events that took place one warm summer night.

All the defense team had to work with were the facts—and the facts were all on the other side. Unless they could somehow raise the dead, their client would most certainly be convicted of murder. It was just a question of degree. If found guilty of first-degree murder, then Cleo Eugene Peters would likely be sentenced to die in the electric chair. "Old Sparky," as the prisoners nicknamed the killing machine, had already taken the lives of more than three hundred others. And some were arguably less deserving then he.

Chapter 6
A VERY SORROWFUL THING

A jury verdict is just a guess—a well-intentioned guess, generally,
but you simply cannot tell fact from fiction by taking a vote.
—William Landay[168]

The state called its first witness Wednesday afternoon. After being sworn in, Sheriff Harry Weiss testified that when he got the call about the shooting on his police radio, he was on his way to Lakeview. He immediately turned his car around and picked up Carl Starner, Millersburg chief of police, before racing on to the Coblentz farm.

When Weiss arrived, he discovered large pools of blood both outside and inside the smaller house—and a dead Amish man on the kitchen floor. "He was laying just inside the door by that cabinet that is to the North or left, facing the door from the inside, and his feet were toward the wall on the west side angling somewhat over to the door that goes into the bathroom," he testified.[169]

Paul Coblentz was flat on his back, with a pillow beneath his head and some wet cloths covering his forehead. There was a hole in his chest and back, as well as his left temple. "Just away from the cabinet on the floor," Sheriff Weiss observed, "there was a five dollar bill laying there all crumbled up."[170]

As far as other signs of violence were concerned, the sheriff confirmed that Dora "had a cut on her lip, and had some scratches and one or two bumps on her head," while the baby "had a few scratches on its face."[171] He also saw that the front of Dora's dress had been ripped down to her waist.

Dusting the stolen truck for fingerprints. *Holmes County Sheriff's Department.*

Weiss related that the truck stolen from the lumberyard was found near the junction by the Saltcreek Township House: "It was in the ditch with the right front wheel and was in an angle and it was headed north, slightly northwest."[172] From there, Paul's killers would have had a clear view of the Coblentz farm, or at least the light in the window of the house.

As they had abandoned the truck, the sheriff assumed that the suspects fled on foot following the slaying. But when he heard about a missing car in Fredericksburg, he was almost certain they had taken it. The two men were later apprehended in Illinois.

Upon arriving in Lacon, Weiss said that he recognized Mike Dumoulin, but it is not clear if that was from his photograph or previous contact. He had arrived with his deputies at about three o'clock in the afternoon and left at eight the following morning. During the trip back to Ohio, Mike and Gene told him about their flight from the Coblentz farm.

"They took over the hills," Weiss testified. "They took out along the highway and when a police car would pass they took to the weeds and that they opened a gate and left out a few horses to go by horse back, but the horses, a whole bunch of them, came out, so they just went on."[173]

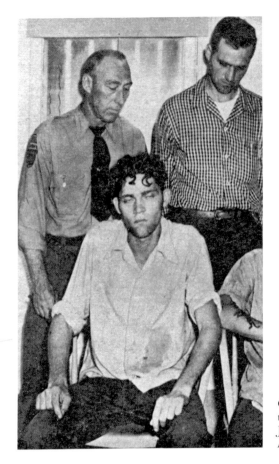

Gene Peters is flanked by (*left to right*) trooper Roy Steinke and Sheriff James Evans. *Holmes County Sheriff's Department.*

Weiss acknowledged that Mose Coblentz had called on Gene Peters at the county jail on July 25, one week after the murder. He insisted that Mose had requested the meeting. According to the sheriff, their conversation went like this:

> *Coblentz: "Did you shoot Paul?"*
> *Peters: "Yes, I did, sir."*
> *Coblentz: "Why did you do it?"*
> *Peters: "Because we needed money."*[174]

Two days later, Sheriff Weiss, James Estill, Dr. Stauffer and Carl Starner, accompanied by court stenographer Luetta Bailey, visited Gene in his cell and asked him if he wanted to make a formal statement. He agreed and wrote out a detailed confession while in their presence.

As is true of many trials, witness testimony provided pieces of the puzzle, but the jurors would have to rely on the prosecution and the defense to explain how they fit into the overall picture. A trial does not necessarily proceed in a linear fashion. It is often like a movie, with many flashbacks.

The purported murder weapon was .25-20 Marlin. It was a lever-action rifle popular with farmers and small game and varmint hunters but not very effective for bringing down large-bodied animals like deer—or man. Its ballistics were "sedate" and the bullets light for fear of splitting the barrel. When fired, it sounded like the pop of a firecracker.

Just before adjournment, James Estill introduced a handwritten confession on four sheets of yellow paper. It was the tenth exhibit for the state. Defense counsel Morgan objected, pointing out that Gene did not have legal representation at the time he wrote it and did not understand his rights. He and co-counsel Anfang also objected to a type-written statement bearing Gene's signature. It purportedly clarified some of the points not fully explained in his handwritten one. Judge Badger said that he would reserve his ruling until later.

During the morning of Thursday, December 5, four witnesses testified before lunch. Sheriff Weiss was the first, called back to the stand to resume his testimony from the day before. On the visit to the crime scene with the jury, Weiss had driven Gene, who sat with him in the front seat, while Ted Geib and Wiley Kendall sat in the back. Weiss asked him how he got the truck stuck in the ditch. Gene purportedly replied that he "was going around forty-five miles an hour when they decided to make a swing around the little intersection and he couldn't turn and got over within two feet of the ditch and then got stopped and put it in reverse and put in the clutch to back up and got the wrong gear and got in second and got in the ditch."[175]

Under cross-examination, Weiss said that he had seen Paul's head wound, taken his pulse and concluded that there was no point in transporting him to the hospital. At six o'clock on the morning following the killing, he had gone to the Holmesville Inn to hear the owner's story of the two strangers who had been there the previous night.

The sheriff's testimony was followed by that of Manning Hunter, Millersburg funeral director, who stated that he had received a call from Edith Weiss, the sheriff's wife, at about 11:15 p.m. She told him to go to the Coblentz farm. Arriving fifteen minutes later, he first went to Mose's home—the big house—where he waited for the coroner to come. He was also present when an autopsy was later performed by Dr. R.C. Harsh, a Mansfield pathologist, and Holmes County coroner Dr. Adam J. Earney.

The intersection at the Saltcreek Township House. *Author photo.*

He then described a problem with "leakage" during the embalming process because the wounds the victim had sustained were so extensive that it was hard to contain the embalming fluids within the body.

Next up was Millersburg police chief Carl Starner, who testified as to the appearance of the crime scene upon his arrival. He had been the chief only since April 15, 1957. Prior to that, he had simultaneously served as a patrolman and a deputy for four or five years. He believed that Weiss had picked him up at about 9:45 p.m., as he was standing on the corner by the police booth in Millersburg. The chief said that they used flashlights to examine the outside of the house, but that wasn't necessary inside because there was an electric light.[176]

Luetta Bailey, court stenographer, was the next witness because Dr. Luther High was not immediately available. She "identified a confession which Sheriff Weiss said Peters wrote and signed in the presence of five persons."[177] After she concluded her testimony, Dr. High took the stand.

Because the county coroner, Dr. Earney, had been unavailable on the night of the murder, Dr. High had responded to a call from Mrs. Weiss. Trained at the Ohio State University College of Medicine, he interned at Massachusetts Memorial Hospital in Boston and then was a surgery resident at the OSU Hospital. He had been a practicing physician in Millersburg since 1934. Although he couldn't recall exactly when he arrived at the crime scene, he calculated it must have been about 12:15 a.m. High had seen Dora at her father-in-law's house, lying on a couch, sobbing.

After High stepped down, Dr. Neven P. Stauffer was sworn in. A physician for twenty-three years, he was educated at Western Reserve University in Cleveland and then interned at St. Vincent's Hospital, Toledo. He also identified himself as the son-in-law of James Estill, the prosecuting attorney. He added little to the testimony.

When Levi J. Hershberger, a plumber, was called to the stand, he identified Gene as the youth who had flagged him down at ten o'clock in the evening on SR 241 about a quarter of a mile from the Coblentz home. Hershberger was accompanied by his daughter, Erma Beechy, and her five children. He stopped so suddenly that one of the children slid off the seat, so he didn't catch the first thing the man said. "All I can remember he said was, 'This truck has to be back in town in an hour' and I told him I couldn't help him and drove off."[178]

Hershberger said that the man, Gene Peters, "smelled strongly of drink," but he was not staggering.[179] He estimated the time was between 9:30 p.m. and 10:00 p.m. He saw the man again two weeks later in the Holmes County Jail. The truck was identified as the property of C.N. Yoder of Millersburg. It "had been stolen while parked at a lumberyard in Holmesville. Authorities maintain Peters and Dumoulin abandoned the ditched truck and made their way to the Paul Coblentz home because it was the only place in the area which had lights burning."[180]

Then it was time for Mose Coblentz, father of the slain man, to testify. The old farmer "spoke slowly and in a low voice, marked by a slight accent. Sorrowfully, he shook his head as he identified a photograph of his son's body at the scene."[181] In life, Paul had never been photographed due to the biblical injunction against "graven images."[182] But in death, he had no say in the matter.

Mose told the court how he was awakened the night of July 18 by the barking of his dog. "Well, I heard him and I heard somebody hollering just after than so we got up and....Got up right away and run over."[183] He estimated it was between 10:30 p.m. and 11:00 p.m. As the he ran to the scene with his wife and daughters following behind, he heard a shot fired from a nearby lane. He didn't know if it was aimed at him or meant to frighten would-be pursuers. He then spotted his son, Paul, lying on the ground in a pool of blood. Standing over the body was Paul's wife, Dora, "screaming hysterically, her dress torn about her waist. Also in the kitchen… the couple's 18-month-old daughter was crying."[184]

Mose Coblentz did his best to cooperate with investigators. *From the* Columbus Citizen, *Scripps-Howard Newspaper/Grandview Heights Public Library/Photohio.org.*

According to Mose, he grabbed a double-mantle gas lantern and immediately ran to Atlee Kauffman's house, about one-third of a mile away, and told him to report Paul had been shot. He then hurried back to the crime scene. His son was still breathing, and "Dora was trying to wash blood away from a wound in Paul's shoulder."[185] She was also fanning him with a book. By the time the officers arrived, however, he was dead.

On July 25, Mose visited Gene in jail, accompanied by Sheriff Weiss and prosecutor James Estill. Contrary to a statement made by Sheriff Weiss in a widely circulated story, he denied initiating the visit or telling the prisoner that he had forgiven him. Speaking to him upstairs through the bars of a turnstile, he asked, "'Did you shoot my son, Paul?' He said, 'yes, sir,' and so, of course, I asked him, 'Did you shoot him twice?' He said, 'yes.'"[186]

"Well, I said, 'I got a big farm and Paul was my standby and he was doing the work there, and I just don't know what to do. It is a very sorrowful thing.'"[187]

According to Mose, Gene replied, "I would do anything to get that boy back if there would be a way."[188]

Paul Coblentz lay mortally wounded on this sidewalk outside his home. *Holmes County Clerk of Courts.*

"As I was leaving," Mose testified, "I said, 'Hope God can forgive you and goodbye to you.'"[189] The visit had taken less than fifteen minutes.

Mose testified for about half an hour. He was the last prosecution witness to be heard before Judge Badger adjourned court until Monday morning due to the scheduled funeral of attorney Morgan's brother-in-law the next day. At that time, the judge would hold a hearing on a motion by the defense in objection to the admission of the written confession. The jury would not be present.

Gene Peters had confessed to the murder in writing—and not just once. It was bad enough there was an eyewitness to the crime without Peters being a witness against himself. The defense lawyers Morgan and Anfang somehow had to get the confessions tossed out. The gist of their argument was that Gene's constitutional rights had been trampled on because he did not have access to an attorney. But the so-called Miranda Warning ruling would not be required by the U.S. Supreme Court until 1966. So, at nine o'clock on Monday morning, December 9, Judge Badger held a hearing outside the presence of the jury to discuss their objections. The key witness would be Gene himself.

The first confession was obtained by authorities in Lacon, shortly after Gene and Mike's arrest on July 21, 1957. The second was written by Gene after he was locked up in Millersburg. For undisclosed reasons, it is the second confession, along with a supplementary question-and-answer statement, that the prosecution sought to introduce into evidence.

According to his attorneys, Gene provided his first confession under duress. They alleged he "was denied food, denied access to legal counsel and promised leniency if he would sign it."[190] As for the second, the four-page handwritten document, they claimed that it was secured only because their client had been tricked into signing the first one. Its existence had actually caught his attorneys off guard. "When one of them turned to the defendant, the latter snapped his fingers and whispered, 'I forgot to tell you about it. I hope it won't hurt the case too much.'"[191]

Mike was purported to be the first to break down after their arrest in Illinois. Gene said that he had been given nothing to eat after his arrest and during the lengthy interrogation. "Declaring that his friend had confessed, an officer is said to have told Peters: 'Your buddy's up there eating hamburgers and drinking coffee. Why don't you wise up and come across?'"[192]

Even if the police had lied to Gene in an effort to obtain a confession, it wasn't illegal. They often play one suspect against the other, and it has been upheld by the U.S. Supreme Court in *Frazier v. Cupp* (1969). They just can't lie under oath. Neither can they employ physical force or misrepresent the suspect's legal rights. And depriving the suspect of food, water, sleep or access to a restroom was walking a thin line in the 1950s.

A parade of witnesses—Stauffer, Starner, Weiss and Bailey—testified that the confession had been signed by Gene. The defendant was then called to the witness stand.

According to Gene, he was interrogated in the presence of seven or eight law enforcement officers in Illinois, some uniformed and some not. They "started shooting questions at me and these highway patrolmen, they pulled out their black jacks and started slamming them in their hands."[193] One examiner even took the sheriff into an adjoining room and said loudly, "I'll see that he talks if you just let me get him by hisself [*sic*]."[194]

Gene related that one patrolman "started telling me this story about a fellow who shot a policeman and got off with five years, he said, you go ahead and talk he said, most likely you will get off the same way."[195]

After being deprived of food and water for a day and a half, Gene said that he was told that he would have to take a polygraph test against his will if he did not confess. So he did. But the situation was different when he was brought back to Ohio.

Under cross-examination, Gene acknowledged that the authorities in Holmes County had neither mistreated nor intimidated him. But he professed that he had been mentally abused because Weiss "kept going over the scene of the crime and things of that sort and trying to make it look as vivid as he could put it across. In other words, trying to make me squirm."[196] As a result, he assumed they would threaten him with a lie detector as well.

Although a paragraph appended to his confession by Estill and signed by Gene stated that he had written his confession without coercion and knowing that he was entitled to legal counsel, he insisted that he only did so because of the Illinois confession and an implied promise of leniency by Sheriff Weiss.

Myron Peters once more made the trip from Iowa to attend the trial. This time, his wife did not accompany him. Owing to the overflow crowd, he was not able to get into the courtroom Monday morning. Every seat was taken, and a score or so of spectators lined the walls. Perhaps one-third of those present were Amish. As the *Sandusky Register* reported, "The plain dark clothing and full beards of the Amish men, who comprise a large part of the community, contrasted sharply with the conventional dress of the others."[197]

"Three times during the day, there were brief recesses when the courtroom lights went out due to blown fuses," Clair Stebbins reported.[198] However, he made no mention of how they occupied themselves while the private hearing was taking place. One person who was not present, however, was Mose Coblentz, who returned to his new home in Florida. In the end, the hearing dragged out so long that it upset the court's schedule, and the jury was given the rest of the day off.

On Tuesday morning, December 10, Gene Peters continued to testify out of the hearing of the jury. He was asked how Sheriff Weiss treated him. "I would say when I first arrived here that the sheriff wasn't too friendly to me....I would say his attitude toward me...oh, just the way he spoke to me and the way he looked at me and things of that sort."[199]

Gene related that he had gone to school as far as the eighth grade before dropping out to join the air force. He completed basic training before he decided to go AWOL. Sentenced to the Federal Correctional Institution in

Ashland, Kentucky, Gene said he spent a year and two months there before being released on January 15, 1957. During that time, he had trained to be a cook. Returning home, he worked on a farm—milking, driving tractors, taking care of stock—and as a gas station attendant. He also worked a week in a canning plant doing cleanup.

Because it would be Gene's only appearance on the stand, the state used it as an occasion for prolonged cross-examination. He testified for five hours. The defense contended that his testimony at the confession hearing did not make him subject to cross-examination before the jury.

When Gene was excused from the witness stand, Sheriff Weiss was called to testify again. "Well, we brought him home from Illinois," he said. "When I took the cuffs off, I said, 'Behave yourself in jail and cooperate with us. It will be easier for you.'"[200]

Having weighed the testimony regarding the confession, Judge Badger finally decided to admit it over defense objections. He then summoned the jury back into the courtroom, and the trial resumed. The state called its final witnesses. Gerald Knapp, proprietor of the Holmesville Inn, identified Gene as the taller of the two young men who had entered the restaurant at 7:10 p.m. on the evening of July 18, 1957, when he was working alone.

The first thing Gerald noticed about them was that the shorter one was carrying a rifle with the lever action open. After placing an order at the bar, they sat down in the first of three booths. Over the next eighty minutes or so, they played the jukebox once or twice and drank four bottles of beer and forty ounces of a sixty-ounce pitcher of 3.2 beer.[201]

Gerald acknowledged that his business had a reputation for selling customers too much alcohol. It was later suggested by the defense that he had downplayed Gene and Mike's alcohol consumption. Asked to estimate the ages of the two men, he "judged the taller of the two to be around twenty-five, the shorter about twenty-three."[202] He was off by six and three years, respectively. As he recalled, they men left sometime after 8:30 p.m. There had been nothing in their conduct to alarm him.

Next to take the stand was Lewis Beech, the proprietor of a Holmesville general store. He stated that he had entered the Holmesville Inn between 7:00 p.m. and 7:30 p.m. While he was sitting at the bar, the two suspects entered, one of them carrying a gun. After they sat down, he left. He guessed that he had been in the tavern no more than fifteen minutes.

Sheriff Weiss then returned to the witness stand yet again. He confirmed that a man from the crime laboratory, a Mr. Wagner, took the photo identified as Exhibit N, which showed the wadded-up five-dollar bill on the floor. He described how he had driven to Illinois on July 23 to pick up the suspects and left the next morning. They arrived in Millersburg between four and five o'clock in the afternoon.

The following day, Mose Coblentz visited Peters in the jail, and the prisoner "confessed" to the shooting. During his time in the Holmes County Jail, Gene wrote letters to his father and a girlfriend. As he had been earlier out of hearing of the jury, Weiss was grilled about the circumstances surrounding Gene's handwritten confession, but he did not waver.

Called back to the stand, Dr. Neven P. Stauffer was also questioned about the confession and whether Gene had asked for an attorney. He was then asked about his examination of the defendant. He said that he took Gene's pulse and learned from the defendant that he had broken his right arm twice but had never sustained any head injuries.

But that was all prologue to the main event.

Chapter 7

THE MOVING FINGER

The Moving Finger writes; and, having writ, moves on.
—Omar Khayyam[203]

Over defense counsel Morgan's objection, prosecutor James Estill took a seat in the witness chair. He then proceeded to slowly read aloud Exhibit J—Gene's handwritten confession—for the benefit of the jury. The document—all misspellings and grammatical errors are original—was dated July 27, 1957:

> *My name is Cleo Eugene Peters, and the following is a sort of summary of the circumstances leading up to the murder of Paul Coblentz by myself. On the 16th of July I received a letter from Mike Dumoulin asking me to come visit him at his home in Wooster, Ohio. I left for Wooster of the same day. I got to Wooster on the 17th about 1:30 in the afternoon wich was about the same time I had left home the day before. When I got to Wooster I went to Mike's address & sat down on a terrice or curb acrosst the street & waited for him to come home from work at about 4:30 he came home & we stood & talked about how good it was to see each other & it had been a long time since we had seen each other. Then Mike told me to go to Hansons restaurant & wait for him & he would be up as soon as he got cleaned up & changed clothes. At about 6:30 Mike came to Hansons & told thear was to be a Homecoming at Shreve & he asked me if I would like to go & I said yes. We then hitchhiked to Shreve. After we had been at Shreve a short*

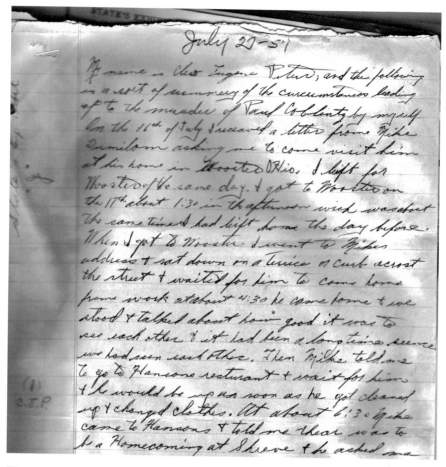

The handwritten confession of Cleo Eugene Peters. *Holmes County Clerk of Courts.*

time we met James Dockerty a friend of Mike's & a few minutes later we met a friend of his whose name I do not know. This boy then told us that if we had a dollar for some gas he would take us to a place to get something to drink. We then started out but just had gotten out of Shreve when he lost controle of the car & we side swiped a bridge & James Dockertry got a cut on the back of his head. About then a lady came by & took Mike, James & I to the doctor, Mike & I left James at the doctors & we went back over to where the celebrations were going on.[204]

About 10:30 or 11:00 we left for Wooster & got their about 12:00, Mike then went home & I went to the Americain Hotel & I got a room under the name of George Anderson. The next day the 18th I again met

Mike about 4:30 & he had his 25-20 rifle with him & he suggested we go ground hog hunting & I said OK with me. We then walked out of town & then took some dirt & gravel roads on wich we walked for some ways. We then met two men in a pickup truck who were also ground hog hunting & they gave us a ride to the highway wich leads to Holmesville, we the & drank a lot of beer. Then at about 9:00 or 9:30 we left walked to the edge of Holmesville & stole a trucke wich ran into the ditch & couldn't get the truck out. We then stopped a car & asked for a ride but it was full of kids & a man & woman. We saw a light at a farm house & decided to go & try & get either some horses or a car. As we got near the house Mike said this must be an Amish farm. We then decided to hold them up & get some money. I went to the door & told the young man who answered I had had a wreck up the road & my friend was hurt & could he take us to town. He then said he would have to ask his father & started acrost the yard to his father's house. Mike then steped out from behind a tree & told him to keep & put up his hands or something to that effect.[205]

He then made him lay down on the grass & Mike went to the house & puled a handkerchief over his face & went in. I then holding a knife on the man took him to the and into the kitchen & made him lay down on the flore spread eagle & asked him whear the money was he said in the sinck drawers & then I opened the drawers & took out about $10.00 from a brown bill fold in it. During this time Mike was talking to the man's wife. The man the asked me if I couldn't leave him some money for he was a poor man so I said yes I could give him some back & I pute a $5.00 bill in his hand. I then steped to the living room door & Mike & I then changed weapons. I gave Mike the knife & he gave me the gun. I then steped back to the kitchen & about this time the man jumped up & started to run out the door. Then I pointed the gun at him & shot him in the back, then levering another shell into the chamber of the gun & catching the empty casing as it came out I ran to the man who was on his hands & knees about halfway out the & shot him in the head on the way out. When we were outside I gave the gun to Mike who fired a shot in the air to keep anyone from following us. We then walked for several miles to Fredericksburg & thear stole a car in wich we drove to Ill at whear we were aprehended.

Signed—Cleo Eugene Peters

H.R. Weiss

Addendum:

92

The above statement was written by me in my own handwriting while alone in my cell on the second floor of the jail on the morning of July 27, 1957, on a tablet and with a pen provided me by the Sheriff. I write and make this statement of my own free will and accord and without having been mistreated, threatened, abused or promised any leniency or reward for making it. I know that it can be used against me in any future court proceeding. I know that I am entitled to counsel and I know that I do not have to make a statement unless I choose to but I do make it so that the true facts will be known.

Cleo E. Peters
Witnessed:

N.P. Stauffer, M.D.
Carl E. Starner
H.R. Weiss[206]

When he had finished, Prosecutor Estill then read Exhibit K—Luetta Bailey's record of the meeting during which the confession was obtained. "Gene, this is pretty much the same procedure you went through in Illinois," Estill had said. "The Sheriff and I read over what you had written this morning. We feel that pretty much is the true story and that is the recollection you have of the happenings."[207] In response, Gene shook his head in the affirmative.

Since Gene would not be taking the stand, this was the only testimony the jury would hear from him. They were his words, but they were coming from the mouth of the man who was seeking his death. So "the climax came Tuesday afternoon when Mrs. Dorie [*sic*] Coblentz, a plain slender young woman wearing gold spectacles and the traditional dark clothes of the Amish sect, pointed to Peters in the courtroom as the man who killed her husband."[208] She was accompanied to the court by her father, Jacob Yoder, with whom she had been living since the murder.

For two hours, the demure young Amish woman was questioned about that terrible night—not only about the details surrounding her husband's death but also the trauma that she and little Esther had experienced. And she responded in a small, quiet, at times barely audible voice. It was a strange position for an Amish woman to be in—to have so much attention focused on her. As newspapers reported, "Spectators in the crowded courtroom strained to hear every word of Mrs. Coblentz's barely audible testimony."[209]

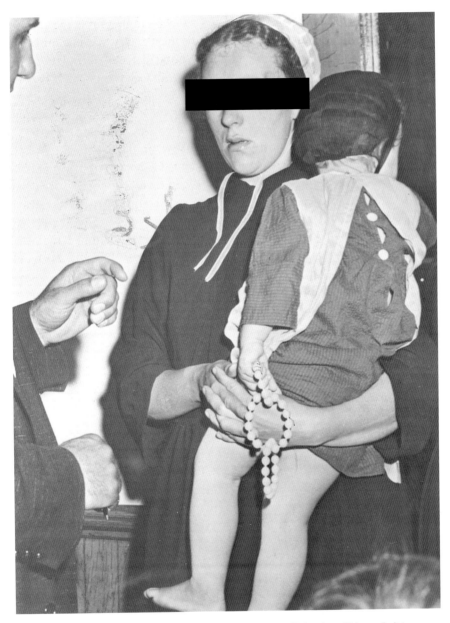

Paul's widow, Dora, holding their daughter, Esther. *From the* Columbus Citizen, *Scripps-Howard Newspaper/Grandview Heights Public Library/Photohio.org.*

Occasionally brushing back a tear, Dora related that she was in the kitchen getting ready for the threshers to come the next day while her husband was eating supper. Upon hearing the dog barking, her husband went to the door. She believed that he went outside, while she went into the bedroom to comfort the baby, who had started crying because the noise had upset her. She could hear talking but could not make out what was being said and made no effort to see who it was.

Then "a light haired short fellow," Mike Dumoulin, came into the kitchen, carrying a knife six to eight inches long. He had a red handkerchief tied around his face, covering his mouth. When he asked whether they had horses, she responded that they did. He then ordered her to go into the living room, adjacent to the kitchen, and sit down.

An archway with curtains separated the two rooms. She took a seat in a rocking chair and continued to hold Esther in her arms. While her husband was still outside, Mike hit her "all over the head and the face and I don't remember everything, but I knew that I was—he hit me awful hard," Dora said.[210] He then cut her on the hand and back with the knife and cut the baby on the head.

A tall man carrying a gun, Gene Peters, then brought Paul into the house. He directed Paul to lie down on the kitchen floor. When he asked him for money, Paul replied that it was in one of the drawers beneath the sink. The tall man searched the drawers and found a brown leather wallet. It contained nine dollars in bills and, perhaps, another dollar in change.

While this was going on, Mike struck Dora several times and threatened to kill her baby if she did not submit to his sexual advances. She screamed for help. The baby was crying, and he told her to keep it quiet. Gene, who had come to the archway, told her to put the baby to bed, but Dora kept holding Esther. The two men then exchanged weapons, with Mike taking the knife and Gene the rifle. Mike told Gene to stand watch. Gene told Dora that he would shoot the baby if she did not put it to bed.

At one point, Gene brought Dora's husband into the living room beside the rocker and had the gun pointed at his neck. "He asked if we had horses. And [Paul] said we had some but that they were turned out and then they took him back to the kitchen again."[211] This was the second time they inquired about horses. Gene then took Paul back to the kitchen.

Mike then proceeded to beat her and tore the front of her dress down to her waist by grabbing the collar and ripping it down. When Dora called out for help, Paul jumped up and charged the door. Although she did not see what happened, Gene shot her husband.

The wadded-up five-dollar bill on the kitchen floor. *Holmes County Clerk of Courts.*

As soon as he heard the shots, Mike left the house. Dora rushed into the kitchen to see what had happened and found Paul lying on the floor, partway out the door. Screaming for help, she tried to drag him back in the house. Failing that, she put a pillow under his head and attempted to staunch the bleeding with cold cloths. When Paul's mother reached them, she tried to give Paul air by fanning him.

Questioned about whether the two men had been drinking, Dora said they did not appear to be under the influence, but they smelled like they had. When asked to identify her husband's slayer, the shy, soft-spoken widow pointed a finger at Gene and said, "That man there."[212]

After Dora's testimony concluded, the state rested its case, and the defense announced that it would call no witnesses. In his closing arguments for the state, prosecutor James Estill cherry-picked the confession to show evidence of a criminal mindset. He noted that Gene had registered at the American Hotel under a false name—George Anderson—in order to disguise his identity. He or Mike had also broken out the back window of the stolen truck

The kitchen door through which Paul Coblentz made a desperate dash for help. *Holmes County Clerk of Courts.*

with the intent of shooting at anyone who pursued them. He also admitted that he knew the Amish were peaceable. One minute, Gene gave Paul five dollars back, the next he killed him. He had calmly caught the "brass"—the empty cartridge from the rifle—so it wouldn't be left as evidence. "Is that the action of an excited man?" he asked the jury.[213]

Attorney Anfang, in his closing arguments, attempted to make two points: that there was no premeditation and that Gene was influenced by his companion. "This boy didn't know who owned the house," Anfang asserted. "He didn't know who would be there. He didn't plan or meditate murder at that time or at any time. He had no malice or hate in his heart for this man. He didn't even know them. He didn't even know where he was."[214] "If you send this 19-year-old to the chair," Anfang pleaded, "some other jury will send an 18-year-old, a 17-year-old or even a 15-year-old boy to his death."[215]

Switching gears, Anfang opined, "I don't mean to stand here and tell you we are blaming Michael Dumoulin entirely for this crime, but I would like for you to consider the influence of Michael Dumoulin. Dora Coblentz says,

'The tall one stood guard,' and I ask you to consider the rest of her testimony along that line."[216] He concluded by saying, "Paul Coblentz is dead. It's over. The moving finger has written. We cannot call him back to life."[217]

Co-counsel Morgan echoed his sentiments. Gene, he said, "is too young to vote, too young to enter into a contract and too young to make a will—yet he is permitted to sign what could be his own death certificate"—referring to his confession.[218] He also pointed out that the death penalty is contrary to the religious beliefs of the Amish. "The prevailing influence, the guiding reason behind this tragedy was this companion, as the prosecutor calls him, Mr. Dumoulin."[219] He went on to say, "He is a young boy, as you know, and young people do foolish and silly things.…Ladies and gentlemen, don't you believe that the determination of the life of this boy would be safer in the hands of God than for us to take that in our hands and decide it?"[220]

Even though it was not directed to him, prosecutor Estill answered Morgan's question. "You are not individual Gods, nor are you twelve together any kind of a God. You judge this case on the facts and circumstances and the evidence."[221] He then concluded with a quotation from the Bible: "How appropriate it would have been for him to have said to his wife and child, 'This is my blood, shed for you,' because that was the fact."[222]

The last word fell to Elmo Estill, who attacked Gene for not taking the stand in his own defense. "It is unfortunate in this particular case that counsel for the defendant stands before you and say, 'We are at a loss to know what happened here—what happened there,' when it would have been so easy for this defendant to have gotten on the witness stand and told you why he did that and why he did that."[223] The former judge then ventured to provide his own answer: "I think you know why he killed. He killed because Paul Coblentz was going for help at the time when the other of these two young criminals was beating and asking the wife time and time again, place the child down, threatening her with a crime, which to a virtuous women, is more horrible than death itself."[224]

The defense objected on the grounds that no evidence had been presented on the subject, but Estill continued: "It was brutal. It was savage. It was inhuman. It was without any iota of mercy. You can take any word I don't care what it is, that would designate this type of an action of a brutal, savage nature and it would fit into the picture in this case."[225]

For three hours and twenty-five minutes on Wednesday afternoon, December 11, the jury of six men and six women deliberated the fate of Cleo Eugene Peters. The female jurors were all housewives and mothers. The male jurors were four farmers, a hardware store clerk and an employee of the Ohio Agricultural Experiment Station.[226] They "had eight possible verdicts from which to choose, ranging from manslaughter."[227]

At 5:20 p.m., they reached agreement: "We the jury find the defendant guilty of murder in the first degree."[228] Specifically, they found him guilty of murder resulting from robbery and deliberate and premeditated murder with malice.

Staring straight ahead and not betraying any sign of emotion, Peters seemed to be waiting for a recommendation of mercy. But there was none. The jurors were then polled, and all affirmed the verdict. So Judge Badger asked Peters to stand. "Mr. Peters, do you have anything to say as to why this judgment should not be pronounced against you?"[229]

"I do not," he replied in a clear voice.[230]

Judge Badger then read the entire 247-word sentence. "His voice choked on the passages which spelled out how electricity was to be applied 'until the same Cleo Peters is dead.'"[231] But Peters did not even wince; he appeared to be the calmest person in the courtroom. Seated in the front row, his father endeavored to suppress his emotions of shock and despair. "His hands were clasped tightly together during the courtroom ordeal."[232]

"Although Peters heard the reading of the verdict stoically," one newspaper reported, "four of the six women on the jury wept when their vote was canvassed and Judge Badger's voice faltered several times when the first sentence was pronounced."[233] By finding him guilty of first-degree murder with no recommendation of mercy, they were mandating a death sentence. Judge Badger immediately sentenced Peters to die in the electric chair on February 11, 1958. Back in his cell, Peters told allegedly told Sheriff Weiss, "I'm glad it's over. I knew sooner or later my crimes would catch up with me."[234]

After a brief farewell at the Holmes County Jail, Myron Peters started to drive back to Iowa that evening. His brother-in-law was with him. His wife, who had remained at home, could not be reached by phone. Presumably, she would learn about the sentence through the radio news broadcasts. The defense had ten days to file a notice for a motion for a new trial. However, prosecutor James Estill had other concerns. He immediately set about preparing his case against Michael Dumoulin, which was scheduled to start on January 13, 1958.

Judge Badger had made one mistake, but it was a big one. He had sentenced Peters to die in the electric chair on February 11, just two months away. But then someone brought to his attention that the law required that a minimum of one hundred days must elapse between the sentence and the execution. So the next day, Thursday, December 12, he called Peters back into the courtroom at 2:19 p.m. for resentencing. He now would be executed on April 10, 1958, giving his counsel two extra months to try to get the verdict overturned. Not surprisingly, attorney Morgan immediately announced that they would appeal. All of Peters's hopes would be riding on a new trial.

The next day, Friday the thirteenth, Peters arrived at the Ohio Penitentiary. Superstitious or not, it had to have been one of the worst days of his life. That evening, the *Columbus Dispatch* editorialized, "The verdict and sentence in the murder trial of Cleo Eugene Peters at Millersburg, Ohio, represent exact and proper justice in this revolting case....By returning the verdict they did, the jury members quite plainly invoked the deterrent effect of the death sentence which is one of the primary reasons for it being written into law."[235]

Chapter 8

THE THREE-JUDGE PANEL

You never know with juries. I'd take a judge every time,
unless of course I was guilty.
—*Kenneth Eade*[236]

Ever since its introduction in 1897 as a more humane replacement for the gallows, "Old Sparky"—the Ohio Penitentiary's electric chair—had been exceedingly busy. Its first victim was William Haas, a seventeen-year-old youth from Hamilton County. Convicted of the brutal murder of Mrs. William Brady, he lost a coin toss to William Wiley. Consequently, he was sent to the chair on April 21, just after midnight. No sooner was Haas's lifeless body removed from the chair than Wiley replaced him, becoming the second victim. Also from Hamilton County, Wiley had been found guilty of killing his wife. Other executions would follow on the average of five a year.

Gene Peters was convicted of first-degree murder—unanimously and without mercy. Unless a miracle happened, he would become the 303rd person to die in the electric chair, including three women. Meanwhile, Mike Dumoulin's attorneys wanted to make certain that he wasn't the 304th.

In preparation for Mike's trial, Isha M. Manley, longtime Holmes County clerk of courts, drew the names of eighty-seven prospective jurors—but they wouldn't be needed. This time, there would be no jury selection because there would be no jury. Forget about trying to establish their client's innocence. Mike's attorneys needed to come up with a persuasive argument for why he didn't deserve the death penalty too. That might take some real lawyering.

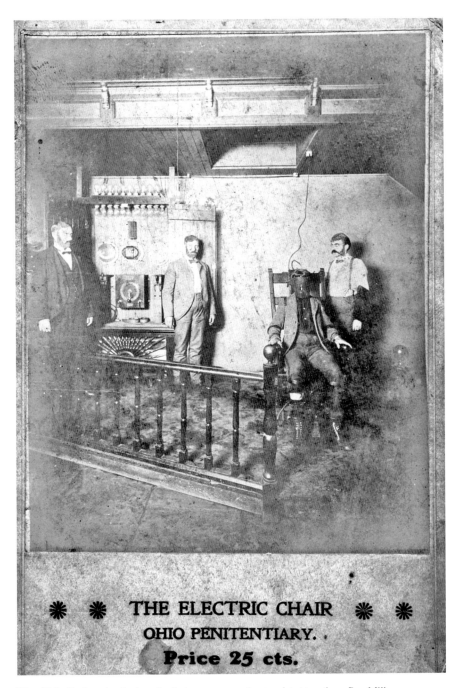

THE ELECTRIC CHAIR
OHIO PENITENTIARY.
Price 25 cts.

The Ohio Penitentiary's electric chair was a popular tourist attraction. *Ron Miller.*

Unwilling to entrust Mike's fate to a dozen local citizens, Wertz and Graven waived a jury trial and agreed for the case to be heard by a three-judge panel appointed by the Ohio Supreme Court. Along with Judge Badger of Holmes County, it included Judge Hugh Emmett Culbertson of Ashland and Judge Lloyd Sanford Leech (sometimes "Leach") of Coshocton. From a legal standpoint, they were a formidable—not to mention elderly—trio.

At seventy-six, Judge Culbertson was the oldest. Born in 1882, he grew up in Milan, Erie County. He began practicing law in Ashland early in the twentieth century and served as the county prosecutor for eight years. During that time, Culbertson was involved in the building of the new courthouse. Some ten years later, he was elected judge and held that post for the next twenty-nine years.

Judge Leech was born in 1887 in Mill Creek Township, Coshocton County. After receiving his law degree in 1912 from Ohio Northern University, he set up practice in Coshocton. For the next fifty-two years, he was a member of the Coshocton County and Ohio State Bar Associations. Leech also served two terms as prosecuting attorney before being elected Common Pleas judge in 1944. He was just about to turn seventy-one.

Judge Badger, who would be sixty in May, was the youngest of the three. He was well acquainted with the facts of the case, having just presided over Gene's trial.

Mike would be represented by William Henry Harrison Wertz and Marion Finney Graven. Born in Wayne County in 1910, Wertz had handled a little of everything in his legal career, except a murder. He also was solicitor for the village of Dalton, which had a population of one thousand or so. At forty-eight, he was the youngest legal mind in the courtroom.

A native of Mochicanville, Ashland County, Graven was born in 1901. When he was two years old, his parents moved to Wooster. Graven attended the local schools, graduated from Wooster College and received a law degree from Ohio State University. In 1929, he became the prosecuting attorney for Wayne County.

After moving into private practice, Graven defended Ernest G. Jones Jr., age twenty-eight, an unemployed construction worker. He had been charged with 1955 murder of Frank Landis, a sixty-seven-year-old farmhand. Landis was stabbed sixteen times with a Scout knife and dumped in a creek. The motive was robbery.

Another court-appointed attorney, Charles C. Jones, resigned from the defense team, declaring that Jones "is insane now and was insane at the time of the crime."[237] However, Lima State Hospital disagreed, and he was convicted of first-degree murder—with mercy. Graven, who was fifty-six and president of the Ohio Association of Election Officials, probably counted that as a win.

Presumably, the three judges would be less swayed by emotions than a jury of Mike's peers. But justice doesn't come cheap. On January 27, 1958, the Holmes County commissioners passed a resolution to move $9,000 from the dog and kennel fund to the general fund. About $5,000 was earmarked for the Peters and Dumoulin trials. The remaining $4,000 was handed over to the agricultural society to buy land.

If Mike's counsel had any second thoughts about asking for a three-judge panel, they were likely dispelled by a headline that appeared in the *Evening Independent* the Saturday before the trial: "Holdup Men Rob Young Amishman."[238]

In an incident eerily reminiscent of the Paul Coblentz affair, a few young men, one brandishing a double-barreled shotgun and the other a pistol, knocked on the door of an Amish farmhouse south of Hartville. They shouted out that their car had broken down and they needed help. When Vernon Coblentz, age twenty, opened the door, they demanded money. He gave them five dollars, but they threatened to knock his father, Noah, on the head if he didn't produce more. So Vernon took another five dollars from his father's wallet and handed it to them as well. He was then forced to stand barefoot in the snow while they made their getaway in a pink 1957 Chevrolet. Fortunately, no one died this time. But the Amish world is a rather small one; the Hartville and Mount Hope Coblentzes were third cousins.

Even before the trial got underway, the newspapers were publishing details about Mike's life. The twenty-one-year-old had "been in and out of trouble since he was in the seventh grade," the *Columbus Dispatch* reported.[239] His first scrape was in August 1951, when he was picked up for breaking into a vacant house. Although no charges were filed, the boy was taken before Probate Court judge Myron T. Brenneman of Wooster, who gave him a reprimand.

Several years earlier, Brenneman told a standing room–only crowd, "Parents are to blame for juvenile delinquency."[240] He made the remarks at a meeting called by the mayor following the arrest of a half-dozen teenage boys who were responsible for twenty burglaries. "One of these boys got a car every time he wanted it," the judge asserted.[241]

Less than a month later, Mike was back in Brenneman's court, charged with stripping an automobile. This time, the judge didn't care for his attitude. He thought that it would be best if the youth were removed from his home

Saint Aloysius Academy became a military school in 1911. *Author's collection.*

and the bad influence of his Wooster associates. His parents readily agreed. "Through the United Catholic Charities," the *Columbus Dispatch* reported, "the judge arranged for his enrollment in an Ohio military academy, with his parents paying the expense."[242] All he needed was a little discipline, they reasoned. Mike spent a year at Saint Aloysius Academy in Fayetteville, which was operated by the Sisters of Charity.[243]

"I kind of straightened up for a while," Mike admitted in retrospect.[244] And if a little bit of military training was good, then more should be better. So he enlisted in the navy late in 1954, serving on the USS *Iowa*. However, it did not prove to be a good fit, and he went AWOL while the ship was docked in Philadelphia. Years later, Mike claimed that the navy "made the penitentiary look good."[245]

Mike's plan was to go to Canada, but he got caught in Ohio on June 1, 1955. "Convicted of stealing an automobile and driving it across a state line, he was sentenced to the federal penitentiary at Ashland, Ky."[246] That was where he met Gene Peters. Evidently, they bonded on some level—two lost souls, perhaps. Mike suggested that it might have been their shared love of hunting and fishing, but he really didn't know.

After serving eighteen months, Mike was paroled in January 1957. He quickly went to work at Record Files Inc. in Wooster, a manufacturer of metal filing cabinets. His father was a foreman there and had worked for the company for five years. Asked whether he enjoyed the job, Mike replied, "Oh, yeah. I always enjoyed working."[247] However, he also kept in touch with

Left: Mike Dumoulin once served aboard the battleship USS *Iowa*. *Jeff Hilton, Wikimedia Commons.*

Right: Sheriff James Evans (*left*) and patrolman John Kelsey flank Mike Dumoulin. *Holmes County Sheriff's Department.*

his buddy Gene and invited him for a visit after he was released. Needing a job and having nothing better to do with his newfound freedom, Gene did—and as a consequence, a man died.

If anything, newspaper coverage of the Dumoulin trial was even less coherent than it had been during the Peters trial. In all likelihood, the reporters did not sit through the whole thing, but rather dropped in from time to time in an attempt to catch up on what they had missed.

When court convened on Monday, February 3, 1958, the first order of business was to visit the crime scene. So, the judges piled into a car and headed off to the Coblentz farm. Upon their return to the courtroom, the prosecution and the defense made their opening statements. After reviewing the crime in detail, Prosecutor James Estill "said Dumoulin was equally as guilty as Peters and should pay with his life."[248] Defense attorney Wentz countered that "although Dumoulin aided and abetted Peters in the crime, the defense would show he should not pay the same penalty."[249]

As the lawyers staked out their positions, Mike, "handcuffed and wearing a green sport jacket and black trousers, appeared calm."[250] He would later say that there wasn't any point in getting worked up over something that was out of his control.

"If Mike had the gun, we would not be here today," Wertz asserted. "He has neither the courage nor the animosity to kill anybody."[251] When the crime was committed, he was living in Wooster "apparently happy and with money in the bank."[252] Anticipating that the state would argue that if Mike had not sent a letter to Peters, the tragedy would not have occurred, Wertz asserted, "At most they will be able to prove him only an aider and abettor."[253]

Despite the fact that the defense was conceding its client's guilt, the panel of judges felt that prosecutor Estill had some explaining to do. "Presiding Judge Wayne W. Badger [*sic*] invited the prosecuting attorney to cite law or legal precedent in support of the visit by [Mose] Coblentz to Dumoulin's cell without knowledge of the defendant's lawyers."[254] It was Graven's contention that he was already Mike's attorney at the time he was brought back from Lacon, Illinois.

According to Mose Coblentz, Sheriff Harry Weiss had invited him to see Mike in jail on July 25, 1957, and not the other way around, as Weiss has previously testified. As it was, they spoke for no more than fifteen minutes while Weiss and Ellis looked on. Mike then wrote out a confession by hand and signed it in the presence of witnesses. The judges temporarily sustained the objection of the defense attorneys to the introduction of his signed confession.

"We could reverse ourselves," Judge Badger told the prosecution, providing a glimmer of hope.[255]

"Sheriff Harry R. Weiss, first prosecution witness, said that prior to the court ruling Dumoulin and Cleo E. Peters, nineteen, of Muscatine, Iowa, had admitted to the attempted robbery and killing."[256] He was followed by Police Chief Carl Starner and Manning Hunter, the undertaker, who testified as to what they saw when they arrived at the crime scene.

There was standing room only in the courtroom the next day, Tuesday, February 4, with many of those standing being Amish. The first witness up was Dora Coblentz. Once again, the young widow bravely took the stand. Dora identified Mike as one of the two men who had invaded their home on the night of July 18, 1957. She referred to him as "the short one" and to Gene as "the tall one."[257]

Unfortunately, the transcript from this trial has not been located. As a result, there is no way of knowing exactly what Dora's testimony was regarding Mike's actions on the night of her husband's murder. However, a baseline can be established from what she testified to in Gene's trial, supplemented by newspaper accounts.

When the dog started barking, Paul answered the door while Dora went into the bedroom to comfort Esther. After her husband stepped outside, she heard "some strange talk."[258] Then "a light haired short fellow," Mike, came into the house carrying a knife, six to eight inches long, in his hand.[259] There was a red handkerchief tied around his face, covering his mouth. He told her to take a seat in the living room, so she sat in a rocking chair still holding the baby.

While Paul was still outside, Mike began to beat Dora, striking her in the face with his hand. "He hit me all over the head and the face," she said, "and I don't remember everything, but I know that I was—He hit me awful hard."[260] He also cut the back of her neck. She screamed for help while the baby cried.

Telling her to "keep quiet," the short man then "cut [her] hand and cut the baby on the head…across the forehead."[261] Some reporters thought she said he had cut a "cross" on Esther's forehead, and at least one described it as an "X."

The "tall man," Gene, then brought Paul into the house. Gene was carrying a rifle and forced Paul to lie down on the floor in the kitchen. He threatened to shoot the baby if Dora did not put her to bed. Mike and Gene then exchanged weapons. Mike "pointed the gun at [her] head" before handing it back to Gene.[262] He then told Gene to watch Paul.

At some point, Gene brought Paul into the living room beside the rocking chair. He had the gun pointed at his neck. Either Gene or Mike asked them for the second time if they had horses. Paul replied that they had some, but they were turned out. Gene then took Paul back to the kitchen and forced him to lie down once more. At this point, Dora said that Mike tore the upper part of her dress down to the waist, revealing her underclothing.

Although Dora heard the shot, she did not see her husband try to flee and did not witness the shooting.

Dora must have described the incident in greater detail during this trial than the first one. And the focus was more on Mike this time. The *Mansfield News Journal* quoted her as saying, "He hit me in the face and took a knife and cut me across the forehead."[263] He then cut the baby on the forehead as well. "It was not deep and did not bleed. He hit me all over."[264]

Dora also purportedly testified that Mike then threated to take the baby out and kill it. "I asked him 'what wrong have I done,'" and he replied, "We have mercy on nobody."[265] The *Holmes County Farmer-Hub*, however, reported that she asked him "if he knew what wrong he was doing"—which isn't quite the same thing.[266]

According to the *Daily Reporter*, Dora claimed that "Dumoulin beat her on the face and back, and threatened to have sexual relations with her… [but] she did not have to submit to the youth."[267] The *Daily Chronicle* reported that testimony brought out that Paul "was slain when he made a dash to obtain help after the intruders beat his wife, Dora, and infant daughter while attempting to rape the young mother."[268] The *News-Journal* quoted Dora as stating that Mike "wanted to have intercourse with me and touched my leg," while also tearing her dress down to the waist.[269] Most of these were not exact quotes, but paraphrases.

The *Times Recorder* wrote that Mike gave officers in Illinois a statement in which he admitted that he "was molesting Mrs. Coblentz and the baby when he heard a shot in the kitchen."[270] However, the *Daily Times*, referencing the statement he gave to Sheriff Weiss, reported that he said "he was in a pantry, filling his pockets with apples after eating some peaches, when he heard a shot."[271]

More than sixty years later, Mike adamantly denied ripping Dora's dress, attempting to rape her or touching the baby in any manner. However, he did admit that when Dora "said something that ticked me off—she said, 'Don't kill me'—I took her glasses off and smashed them."[272]

When he heard Gene fire the rifle, Mike recalled, "I about puked. Had no idea he would do anything like that."[273] Catching up with Gene in the doorway, he took the rifle away from him. "I thought about shooting him in the leg and waiting until the sheriff got there," Mike recalled. "I wish I would've, now."[274] He said he did the same thing after Gene shot the constable in Illinois. "There's not a day goes by that I don't think of that. And how stupid I was."[275] Of course, Mike said none of this in court because he did not testify.

Dora's story wasn't one that George and Emma Dumoulin wanted to hear. "Anxiety and agony" were etched on their faces."[276] His grandparents Mr. and Mrs. Ross Giaugue of Millersburg and an aunt were also in attendance.

"We can't understand it," said Mrs. Dumoulin when court recessed. "Michael isn't a mean person"—a sentiment echoed by the parents of many wayward children all the way back to Adam and Eve.[277] Sighing, she then added, "But it happened—and we know it happened."[278] According to his mother, he had been "emotionally disturbed" for many years. "We couldn't find out what was the trouble. He needed help but no one knew what to do."[279]

When Mike returned home and went to work with his father, his parents wanted to believe that he had changed for the better. She still clung to the belief that he was a good boy. "I'm sure it was the drinking," she said. "He was not himself."[280] But maybe, in truth, he was himself. Maybe he was the bad influence. "I thought he had adjusted so beautifully," said the mother. "It's so sad."[281]

Dr. High was the second witness of the day. In addition to declaring Paul dead, he had "treated Mrs. Coblentz for hysteria, but…did not examine her for wounds or bruising."[282] Neither did he mention any marks on her face.

Mose Coblentz was the final witness for the day. He "testified he was in bed when he heard a farm dog bark and then heard shots and his daughter-in-law scream."[283] He, his wife and two daughters immediately ran to his son's home and found him in a pool of blood. Dora was screaming so hysterically that they couldn't talk with her. Paul was breathing, but that was all. The life was ebbing out of him.

When shown a crime scene photograph of his slain son—eyes closed, skin gray, lying on his back and shirtless—Mose cried, "Oh, that's so natural," as the tears rolled down his cheeks.[284] It was just the second time he had seen the photograph—the only one of Paul ever taken. "Oh my, why must a man go through this again?"[285]

Seated fewer than twenty feet away from the witness, Dumoulin appeared to be on the verge of tears as he watched the grieving father's sobs. As Mose stepped down from the witness stand, the accused rubbed his eyes. Mose was not cross-examined by the defense. It had been an emotional day.

Chapter 9

THE LUNGS OF LIBERTY

Representative government and trial by jury are the heart and lungs of liberty.
—*John Adams*

Court was in recess on Wednesday, February 5, to allow for two witnesses—William Abernathie and Thomas B. Howerton—to make the drive from Springfield, Illinois.

On Thursday, the fourth and final day of Mike's trial, the prosecution called Abernathie and Howerton to the stand. Both men were employed by the Illinois Bureau of Criminal Identification and Investigation. They had been summoned to provide testimony regarding the confession Mike made while in Illinois custody. Apparently, that confession suited the prosecution's case better than the one obtained in Ohio.

Howerton, age fifty-six, had retired as a detective sergeant from the Springfield Illinois Police Department in 1953 following thirty-one years of service. He was immediately appointed chief investigator at the bureau by Illinois governor William G. Stratton. Abernathie was also an investigator at the bureau, often teaming up with Howerton. His particular expertise was ten years as a Keeler polygraph operator. This was a brand of polygraph marketed by Leonarde "Nard" Keeler. Recognizing its financial potential, Keeler had established the first testing protocol, made the device portable and founded a polygraph school.

However, the reliability of "lie detectors" was largely a matter of faith. The first empirical study of the polygraph wouldn't be undertaken until 1965.

As the U.S. Committee on Government Operations concluded, "There is no lie detector, neither man nor machine. People have been deceived by a myth that a metal box in the hands of an investigator can detect truth or falsehood."[286] Consequently, polygraph results are not generally permitted to be introduced in court.

Both Abernathie and Howerton testified concerning the contents of a statement Mike made on July 23, 1957, and the circumstances under which it was obtained. Both men asserted that "no pressure or coercion was placed on Dumoulin to make the statement."[287] Abernathie insisted that Mike "was accorded all privileges, including those of obtaining counsel and notifying his parents."[288] He was under no duress but had been fed and permitted to rest before being interrogated.

The two men had questioned Mike at the request of Sheriff Jay Evans "with no one else present."[289] The result was a seven-page statement in which he admitted "being in the Coblentz home when the farmer was shot."[290] Although Mike was told at one point that he would have to submit to a polygraph test, there was no indication this occurred.

Despite defenses objections, the signed confession was entered as an exhibit, and portions were read aloud in court.

Lacon, Illinois
July 23, 1957
Marshal Co. Court House
3 p.m. D.S.T.

"Statement of Michael Dumoulin"[291]

My name is Michael Dumoulin and my age is 20 years. I am single and I live with my parents, Mr. and Mrs. George Dumoulin at 1122 Lincolnway West, Wooster, Ohio. I finished High School while I was in the Navy, however, I have an undesirable discharge from the Navy.

I make the following statement of my own free will and accord. I have not been mistreated, threatened, abused or promised any lieniency in order to get me to make this statement. I know that any statement I make will be used against me at a future court proceeding. I know that I am entitled to counsel and I know that I do not have to make a statement unless I choose too. I am willing to waive extradition to the state of Ohio where I am wanted on the charge of murder as an accessory to the murder committed by Cleo Peters Thursday, July 18, 1957.

The distance from the Saltcreek Township House to the Coblentz farm. *Author photo.*

On Wednesday July 17, 1957, as I returned from work from the Record Files Incorporated about four thirty p.m., Cleo Peters was waiting for me and he asked me to go to the Homecoming which was held or was being held at Shreve, Ohio. I told Cleo I would as soon as I dressed. Cleo left and I told him I would meet him at Hanson's restaurant after I finished dressing and cleaning up. I went to town and met Cleo at Hanson's restaurant.

The two of us then started hitchhiking and we caught a ride and arrived in Shreve, Ohio, about seven o'clock p.m. About eight thirty p.m., James Dockerty, Cleo Peters, and I were riding with a boy whom James knew to Big Prairie, Ohio, to get something to drink and on the way we had a wreck. This boy who was driving sideswiped a wooden bridge and a lady came by and took James, Peters, and I into Shreve, Ohio, to a doctor's office. Cleo and I then left Shreve, hitchhiking back to Wooster, Ohio. We arrived back in Wooster near midnight. Cleo then asked me if I would go ground hog hunting with him the next night after I got off from work and I told him I would and Cleo went to the American Hotel to stay all night.

The following day, Thursday, July 18, 1957, I worked all day and came home about four thirty p.m. I went in and changed my trousers and picked up my .25-.20 rifle and a box of shells and I told my folks I was going ground hog hunting. I walked down to the sweet shop located on old

Mansfield road and U.S. Highway 30 and met Cleo Peters, we started walking on route 250 by the Wooster Township School, then walked down a dirt road and walked about four miles on a dirt road and two fellows who were ground hog hunting picked us up and took us to Ohio route 76. Then we walked into or caught a ride into Holmesville, Ohio.

When we got to Holmesville we went to the Holmesville Inn. We arrived there before dark and we drank beer until 9:30 p.m. or ten o'clock p.m. The two of us drank eight or ten pitchers of beer together. We then left Holmesville Inn, and we stole a logging truck. I believe the make of the truck was an International. Cleo drove the truck. We drove the truck to Benton, Ohio, and started on the road to Mt. Hope, Ohio. When we got to the township house, we decided to turn around and go back to Millersburg, Ohio, but in turning around Cleo ran the truck in a ditch. We tried to get the truck out of the ditch but couldn't.

We saw a house about a thousand yards away with the light burning. We took my rifle from the truck and I carried it. Cleo was carrying my bowie knife in his belt. We walked up to the house with the intention of stealing a couple of horses to ride back to Wooster. I could tell that this was an Amish house and I believe this Amish man's father lived there too as there was two houses right close together.

When we got to the house, Cleo went to the door and knocked on the door. I stood in the yard a few feet away with the rifle. When the Amish man came to the door, Cleo told him that we had a wreck and his buddy was hurt. The Amish man stepped out of the house into the yard. Cleo told the man to lay down on the ground. The Amish man laid down and Cleo was holding the knife to his throat and I then walked up and I gave Cleo the gun and I took the knife from Cleo. I walked into the house and a young man woman was standing at the stove with a small baby in her arms warming milk for the baby. She asked me what I wanted and I told her I wanted something to eat. She said to go to the pantry and get it. I went to the pantry and ate some peaches. About this time Cleo brought the Amish man into the house and made him lie down on the floor. Cleo told him to lay still and he wouldn't get hurt. The lady of the house said take anything you want but don't hurt Paul or any of us. Cleo then looked through the chest of drawers or the cabinet sink.

I was filling my pockets with applies in the pantry. I heard a shot and I ran out of the house and this Amish man was laying just outside of the door and he was on his hands and knees trying to get up. I jumped over him and I heard peat [likely "Pete"—short for Peters] *or Cleo eject or throw another shell into the barrel of the rifle. I then heard another shot and Cleo came running and said he had killed him. I asked Cleo why he killed him and he said he got up and started to run and that was when he shot him. After Cleo shot him, I heard his wife scream and I heard other people screaming and I that* [likely "thought"] *that was his parents coming from the other house close by.*

After we left the house we walked on a dirt road and stole two horses and road them into Wayne County and turned them loose. We then walked into Fredericksburg, Ohio, and we found a 1956 Pontiac two door sedan with the keys in it. The car was parked near a bridge by the side of a house.

Cleo drove the car first but I drove the car part of the way through Indiana and Illinois on our way to Musatine, Iowa, where Cleo lived. On our way back to Illinois, we traveled back roads we heard on the radio that the police were looking for the car we had stolen on our way back we hid the car in a barn all day and traveled at night. We were both arrested by the Illinois State police after we had abandoned the car north of Lacon, Illinois, at a road junction near Toulon, Illinois, July 22, 1957.

I have read and had the about statement read to me and it is true and correct.

Michael A. Dumoulin
Witnesses
Wm. Abernathie
Thomas Howerton[292]

Significantly, Mike made no mention of molesting Dora or her baby, despite reports to the contrary.[293] And his admission that they consumed "eight or ten pitchers of beer" suggests that alcohol may well have been a factor in the crime, although he would maintain that it wasn't.

Both sides rested in the morning, the state at 10:40 a.m. and the defense just twelve minutes later. Attorneys Wertz and Graven had neither called any witnesses nor placed their client on the stand. The three-judge court overruled a defense motion of a directed verdict of acquittal, clearing the way for closing arguments to begin that afternoon. Judge Badger granted each side ninety minutes for summation.

In the closing arguments, attorney Elmo Estill said that Mike was not deserving of sympathy. Defense attorney Wertz countered, "The prosecution by asking the death penalty is asking more than the widow or the family or the bishop of the church to which Paul Coblentz belonged."[294] Attorney

Graven concluded by quoting Shakespeare's *Merchant of Venice* speech in which Portia states, "The quality of mercy is not strained."[295] It was a request for compassion and forgiveness.

The verdict was delivered late Thursday afternoon, one hour and thirty-seven minutes after Judge Badger and his fellow jurists commenced deliberation. They found Mike Dumoulin not guilty on the first count (murder by premeditation) but guilty on the second (murder while committing a felony). The court took into consideration his claim that he was in another room when Coblentz was shot and that he had asked his co-defendant, "Why did you do it?"[296]

As Judge Badger read the verdict, "A thin, clean-cut looking youth tapped his foot nervously today as he heard himself ordered to life imprisonment for his part on the wanton slaying of a young Amish farmer last summer."[297] There were an estimated 250 people gathered in the courtroom, including 40 Millersburg High School seniors who were there for a living civics lesson.

"Sentenced to life imprisonment as an accessory in the July 18, 1957, slaying of Paul Coblentz, Amish farmer, 20-year-old Michael Dumoulin" would likely be eligible for a reduced sentence after twenty years or so.[298] It had been a victory for the defense.

Seated on either side of Mike were his parents, Mr. and Mrs. George Dumoulin. "The mother broke into tears at the verdict. The father's face became red and tears were in his eyes."[299]

Satisfied with the sentence, Wertz and Graven said that they would not be filing an appeal. While returning to his cell, Mike purportedly said, "I feel I had a fair trial and I'm satisfied with the verdict."[300] His mother said, "Our prayers have been answered," while his father commented, "I am glad it came out this way."[301]

That same day, Dr. Luther High was appointed assistant coroner by the Holmes County commissioners. He would be paid ten dollars per month for one year. Perhaps the trial had been his audition for the job.

Mike was delivered to the Ohio Penitentiary by Holmes County sheriff Harry Weiss on Friday, February 7, 1958. At the time, there were ninety-nine prisoners serving life sentences in the Ohio Penitentiary. Although he would be joining his partner-in-crime, Gene, they would not be housed in the same unit. Gene, after all, was sitting on Death Row awaiting execution.

Chapter 10

LIFE ON DEATH ROW

*If Jesus had been killed twenty years ago, Catholic school children would be
wearing little electric chairs around their necks instead of crosses.*
—*Lenny Bruce*[302]

It used to be that friendships made on Death Row were, by their very nature,
brief. Justice was surprisingly swift. From arrest to trial typically took less
than a year and from sentence to execution about another year, including the
appeals process. While it might be harsh to call it perfunctory, it was efficient.
And if mistakes were made, it was more likely due to perjured testimony and
official misconduct than simply a matter of haste. When innocent people
were executed, it could usually be traced back to bias or corruption.

Capital punishment had been part of the criminal justice system in Ohio
since before it became a state in 1803. At first it was public hangings staged
in the county where the crime occurred. Then in 1885, the state legislature
passed a law requiring that all executions be performed within the walls
of the Ohio Penitentiary and outside public view. But following a series
of badly botched hangings, including a decapitation, there was a renewed
outcry against the gallows.

The death penalty was given a new lease on life with the introduction of the
electric chair—ostensibly a more humane and expedient, if no less revolting,
killing machine. After a few unfortunates appeared to be cooked rather than
electrocuted, however, the protests resumed. Capital punishment continued
to be a polarizing issue even as the penitentiary's death row was filling up.

Some academics would later discover an inverse relationship between the decline in extrajudicial lynchings and the increase in legal executions—fewer lynchings correlated with more executions.

While Cleo Eugene Peters—no. 103851—was sitting on Death Row, the debate over capital punishment was being driven by the case of Caryl Whittier Chessman. In January 1948, Chessman was sentenced to death for a series of crimes committed in the Los Angeles area. A convicted robber, kidnapper, rapist and all-around sociopath, he became a cause célèbre as a consequence of four best-selling books he wrote in prison—the last three smuggled out. The first, *Cell 2455, Death Row*, was turned into a movie, although his character was renamed "Whit Whittier." Promoted as the "Times, Crimes and Confessions of the Lover's Lane Bandit," the film was less than flattering.

What made the Chessman case so controversial was that he had been sentenced to death for a kidnapping in which nobody died. Following the abduction of the Lindbergh baby, California passed a law that allowed for the death penalty to be imposed even if the kidnapping did not involve bodily harm. Whether Chessman had kidnapped his victims was open to debate. But what wasn't was that this career criminal was a skilled writer who professed his innocence. And many people wanted to believe him.

There was a worldwide movement to spare Chessman from the gas chamber, in addition to a heightened debate over capital punishment in general. The author, though, was not exactly the ideal poster boy for changing people's minds on the issue. As he had once said of himself, "I am not generally regarded as a pleasant or socially minded fellow."[303] So, after nearly twelve years on Death Row, the improbable media darling died in the San Quentin gas chamber on May 2, 1960.

For Gene, the big question, as always in capital punishment cases, was whether he would actually be executed. And he wouldn't have to wait twelve years to find out. At the time, death sentences were not at all uncommon, although they were somewhat arbitrary. Black people were more likely to be sentenced to death than white and poor people more likely than rich. Cells on death row—the Ohio Penitentiary had seven—were sometimes at a premium. But the likelihood of the death sentence being carried out was something of a crapshoot, especially if the governor was conflicted about capital punishment, as many increasingly were.

C. William O'Neill was Ohio's governor when Gene was convicted of the Coblentz murder. During the period of 1950–59, he and his two predecessors—Frank J. Lausche and John William Brown—commuted twenty-two death sentences. But it wasn't a sure thing. O'Neill's successor, Michael V. DiSalle, whose opposition to the death penalty would, arguably, sabotage his political career, famously observed, "I found that the men in death row had one thing in common: they were penniless."[304] Gene was one of them.

Gene had been sitting on Death Row since shortly after his trial ended in December. His attorneys, Raymond Morgan and William Anfang, had immediately set about preparing an appeal. But first they had to obtain a stay of execution so he wouldn't die as scheduled on April 10, 1958. It was a lot of responsibility for the two lawyers. They held his life in their hands. But all indications are they took it seriously and did their best. Still, preparing an appeal took time—and time was at a premium.

A little more than three weeks after he arrived at the Ohio Penitentiary, Gene "experienced" his first execution. On the third day of January 1958, Norman Walker, age thirty-two, was the first person to die in what would prove to be a busy year. It's not known how Gene reacted, but typically it was a somber occasion on Death Row and in the prison generally. Given his demeanor during his trial, he probably showed little emotion.

In all of 1957, only one prisoner was executed in Ohio: Harold Shackleford. He had killed a Newark woman, Mary Dunne, while she was on her way to church. As Robert Weaver, Shackleford's attorney, observed, "Psychiatrists say he is legally sane, and I agree, but I do think there is something wrong with his make up somewhere. His death cannot remedy the crime."[305] But his argument was lost on Governor O'Neill, who chose not to contravene the will of the court in his first death penalty case.

Neither did O'Neill spare Norman Walker. While on parole, Walker had kidnapped his girlfriend, Rosie Sustarsic, after she left a tavern. Garner M. Robertson, a part-time police officer in the Cleveland suburb of Valley View, was approaching Walker's parked car when he was struck with a fatal shotgun blast.

"I wish there was some way I could…turn the clock back," Walker said. "I never consciously intended to kill anyone."[306] But he had. As he was seated in the electric chair, the condemned man "broke his stoic expression by turning and winking at Warden Ralph W. Alvis," one of sixteen witnesses, just before the hood was pulled over his head.[307]

Considered a progressive when it came to prison reform, Alvis, known as "Big Red," had been warden at the Ohio Penitentiary since 1948 and was an outspoken critic of capital punishment. He is credited with implementing major reforms, including the elimination of the silent system, lock-step march

Alvis House was named after Ohio Penitentiary warden Ralph W. Alvis. *Gloria Nielsen Iannucci/Alvis.*

and striped clothing. Alvis inspired David Dunning, an Episcopal priest who taught Bible studies at the prison, to open a halfway house. Alvis House, as it would be called, was set up to help newly released inmates transition to life outside the prison.[308]

A week following Walker's execution, attorneys Anfang and Morgan claimed that there had been a dozen errors made during Gene's trial. In moving for a new trial, they charged that "Judge Badger erred in overruling motions, permitting irregularities in courtroom conduct, procedures and questioning and charged Prosecutor James Estill with misconduct."[309] It was the opening volley in the first battle for what would be a yearlong war waged on behalf of their client.

Life on Death Row varied somewhat from inmate to inmate, but generally it resembled the experience of Hocking County wife-slayer Ben Meyer. Meals were delivered to his cell three times a day—at 8:00 a.m., 11:00 a.m. and 3:00 p.m. From 7:30 a.m. to 2:15 p.m., he could exercise in the corridor in front of the seven death cells, but the time had to be divvied up between him and the other inmates on Death Row. "The remainder of his time is spent in his cell, with its fold-up bunk and its toilet without a seat."[310]

Meyer could read—novels from the prison library, magazines such as the *Saturday Evening Post* or the Bible—or listen to the in-house radio broadcast through earphones. However, much of the time he thought about his crime, trying to figure out what sent him into a blind rage that resulted in the killing of his wife. Not surprisingly, a number of Death Row inmates went mad under these conditions.

Gene told a reporter that he was spending most of his time on Death Row reading historical novels and science fiction, writing letters and listening to the radio. He exercised fifteen minutes a day by walking back in forth in front of the Death Row cells. During his first six months in prison, he had just two visitors: his attorney and Reverend Walter E. Johnson, a Calvary Baptist minister from Muscatine. Although Johnson only visited once—likely due to the distance and, possibly, poor health—they were corresponding regularly.[311] "He said he has given more thought to religion since he came here in December."[312]

An aerial view of the Ohio Penitentiary. *From the* Columbus Citizen-Journal, *Scripps-Howard Newspaper/Grandview Heights Public Library/Photohio.org.*

The various moods of Sam Sheppard during his trial. *From the* Columbus Citizen, *Scripps-Howard Newspaper/Grandview Heights Public Library/Photohio.org.*

Many Death Row inmates wrote letters and often would write back to anyone who wrote them one. Before he was put to death on November 26, 1956, for the kidnapping and murder of Shirley Bradford, a twenty-nine-year-old Fremont, Ohio waitress, Samuel W. Tannyhill claimed that he had received more than one thousand letters since he was sentenced to die—some from as far away as Japan."[313]

While Gene wrote to his parents on a regular basis, they had yet to visit due to the distance involved. It is quite likely that he received his share of unsolicited letters as well, since there are a surprising number of women who find the prospect of a relationship with a convicted killer irresistible. One such woman was Ariane Tebbenjohanns, a German divorcée, who initiated a relationship with Dr. Samuel Sheppard, the prison's best-known inmate. He was convicted—and eventually acquitted—of the murder of his wife, Marilyn. Three days following his release in 1964, he and Ariane married.

Only a week after Walker went to the chair, Robert W. Mohrhaus followed. Known as the "Strawberry Killer," Mohrhaus, age twenty-two, was "executed for the burglary slaying of Mrs. Leona McCrocklin, 71, in her Cincinnati flat." His take was fifteen dollars. Right after stabbing the elderly woman to death, he sat down and ate a bowl of strawberries. For his last meal, Warden Alvis saw that Mohrhaus was served fresh orange juice, shrimp and anchovy cocktail, roast duck with oyster dressing, baked Idaho potato, pineapple and cream cheese salad, Neapolitan ice cream, hot buttered rolls and preserves, goat's milk, coffee and—of course— strawberry shortcake.

On February 28, 1958, thirty-one-year-old James E. Vaughns of Cuyahoga County was electrocuted for the rape and murder of Dianne Buckhanon, a seventeen-month-old baby. This was not the type of crime that generated much sympathy. Not surprisingly, Governor O'Neill declined to interfere with the scheduled execution of a baby rapist. "He went to the electric chair, mumbling the Lord's Prayer," the *Columbus Dispatch* reported.[314]

The prisoners on Death Row were not the only ones affected by the executions. Major Grover Powell, who spent thirty-one years at the penitentiary, told a *Dispatch* reporter, David Lore, "Nobody ever really wanted to work the executions, nobody ever volunteered."[315] Such duties as supervising the prisoner during the last meal, strapping him (or, occasionally, her) into the chair and pushing the buttons were rotated. The warden was authorized to split seventy-five dollars in overtime pay among the attending officers, but some refused it.

Although capital cases were hardly their specialty, Morgan and Anfang were determined to do their best. The public defenders' first order of business was to buy some time. On March 5, 1958, they did just that when Judges C.B. McClintock of Canton, Dean McLaughlin of Massillon and Robert B. Putnam of Millersburg—the Fifth District Court of Appeals— "stayed the electrocution, set for April 10, to allow time for consideration of an appeal."[316] Less than three months later, however, the court denied the appeal. A new execution date was set for September 8, 1958.

In death penalty cases, it is advisable for an inmate to appear contrite. Whether it was calculated or sincere, Gene had begun doing that almost as soon as he was arrested. "I was pretty much of a fool getting into a mess of this sort," he told reporter Bernard Butler.[317] As far as the death sentence hanging over his head, he admitted, "I think quite a bit. There's not much else to do....I don't know why I did it....I do a lot of things on the spur of the moment without thinking....We were a little drunk at the time, but I had no idea it would turn out the way it did."[318]

Asked why he shot the young farmer, Gene said, "I guess I was scared and nervous"—not the best of excuses, but an understandable one.[319] While he said his parents were "pretty broken up about what happened," he wasn't particularly nervous about his fate.[320] "I'm just looking for the worst and hoping for the best. I could say I hope I'll get a life sentence like Dumoulin."[321]

On July 1, 1958, the Ohio Supreme Court received the appeal from Morgan and Anfang that claimed there were procedural errors in his trial. There were always procedural errors, of course, but they had to be of some consequence to disrupt the wheels of justice. Nevertheless, this bought them a postponement until November 7 while the Supreme Court reviewed the case.

Six days later, Lemuel Trotter, age thirty-one, and Robert Lee "Hambone" Jackson, forty-one, were executed just a few hours apart for the slaying of off-duty detective Walter Hart during an attempted robbery. Both men were from Cincinnati. Jackson had originally been sentenced to death in 1956 but was granted several stays of execution. Trotter wasn't captured until February 1957. A third suspect, Willie Barnett, who was also captured at the time, escaped the death penalty when he was committed to the Lima State Hospital for the Criminally Insane.

Three months later, on October 7, 1958, the Ohio Supreme Court rejected Gene's appeal, so it was back to the drawing board for Morgan and Anfang. The execution would go ahead as scheduled just one month away. The next step was to apply to the Ohio Pardon and Parole Commission for executive clemency. More paperwork. This time, they argued that Gene's sentence should be the same as that of his codefendant, Mike Dumoulin.

Although Gene Peters and Walter J. Byomin were in proximity on Death Row, they probably were not close friends. And yet they had two things in common: they both were convicted murderers, and they both were scheduled to die on November 7, 1958. The commission heard both of their appeals during the same session.

Byomin had been convicted of the fatal shooting of Special Officer Edmund D. Smith in Wellington, Ohio. His attorneys argued before the commission that he didn't know Smith was a policeman, but premeditation wasn't a consideration under the law.

Prosecutor James Estill told the commission "he believed Dumoulin was the more guilty even though Peters was the triggerman. He said Dumoulin's attempt to molest Dora Coblentz caused her to scream, distracting Peters guarding her husband."[322] Although he believed that justice had been served, his "personal feeling [were] another thing."[323]

Morgan and Anfang weren't the only ones trying to save Gene's life. Throughout their history, the Anabaptists have opposed capital punishment. They believe that "if given time, every human being may at some point

Above: At Lima State Hospital, patients were evaluated by a team of mental health professionals. *Authors' collection*.

Right: At the Ohio Penitentiary, guards conducted frequent searches for contraband. *Authors' collection*.

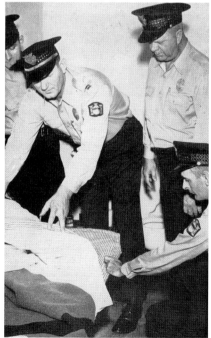

reach a place of real repentance and turn to God."[324] But that was more in the abstract, not in reality. Then one of their own was murdered. As Stephen Russell observed, "Rarely had the issue [of capital punishment] been so immediate for the Amish."[325]

The Amish firmly believe that those who commit crimes should suffer consequences. Furthermore, they recognize the state's authority to prosecute them under the law. That was why Paul Coblentz's widow and his father agreed to testify in both trials. But neither could they turn their backs on Gene Peters once he was sentenced to death. As an Amish man from Ontario put it, "Will we as Amish be left blameless in the matter if we do not present a written request to the authorities, asking that his life be spared?"[326] It wasn't a rhetorical question. It was a call to action.

In 1958 alone, forty-eight men were put to death in the United States—gassed, hanged or electrocuted—an average of four per month. Over the better part of a year, the Amish and Mennonites deluged the offices of government officials, up to and including the governor of Ohio, with letters and petitions, asking for a stay of execution. As Levi Miller later wrote, "The case was lifted up for the nonresistance of the Amish and Mennonites in not wanting the state to kill a man in their name."[327]

The ministry began organically with the Amish simply being Amish. When Gene's parents came to Ohio for the trial, the Amish approached them as "fellow victims of their son's actions" and invited them into their homes for dinner.[328] It continued with letters, petitions and discussions in Amish and Mennonite newspapers on the topic of capital punishment and the Peters case in particular.

While the trials of Gene and Mike were unfolding, Levi Miller recalled that "our Holmesville School which sometimes showed movies during the noon hour showed a black and white documentary of the Ohio State Penitentiary and the electric chair."[329] Following Gene's conviction, Reverend Paul Hummel of the Berlin Mennonite Church took several Amish ministers and even members of the Coblentz family to the Ohio Penitentiary to visit the condemned man. Eventually, petitions signed by 150 Holmes County residents, both Amish and non-Amish, asking for mercy were presented to Governor O'Neill by attorney Morgan.

Having received the pardon and parole commission's secret recommendation, Governor O'Neill weighed Gene's request for clemency and granted it on November 7, 1958—nine hours (some sources say seven or eight) before he was to take the last walk to the death house. O'Neill felt that Peters and Dumoulin were equally guilty under the law, so his sentence was commuted to life imprisonment. "The governor's press secretary, Hal Conefry, said the action was taken following a thorough study of all aspects of the case."[330]

Governor O'Neill was born in Marietta, Ohio, in 1916 and graduated from the Ohio State University College of Law in 1942. After serving as a state representative and Speaker of the House, he was elected state attorney general in 1950 at the age of thirty-four. He resigned that position in 1957 when he was elected governor of Ohio.

It was only the second commutation O'Neill had granted since he took office two years earlier. "Peters was sitting on the floor of his cell in death row when the prison chaplain took him word that his life had been saved. His head dropped between his knees and he began sobbing."[331] After regaining his composure, he said, "Thank Governor O'Neill for me."[332]

"A few minutes before he learned his death sentences had been commuted, Gene only picked at his food. But after being removed from death row into the prison hospital, he ate a big fish dinner."[333] Earlier, he had said that he was "resigned to go."[334] Although prosecutor James Estill told Governor O'Neill that he felt the trial had been properly conducted and the sentence was just, he declined to voice an opinion, public or private, regarding the commutation.

"My life is straighter than it ever has been before," Gene told a reporter, crediting prison chaplain Clarence Swearingen for setting him "straight."[335] Swearingen, age sixty-five, was a Methodist minister who had served at various churches throughout Ohio, including Middleport, Delphos, Circleville, London and the Third Avenue Church in Columbus.

One week later, O'Neill spared two more inmates. Joseph and Bert Buza, ages twenty-one and seventeen, respectively, had been convicted of murdering Margaret Denham, an elderly woman, in Burton, Ohio. Because the brothers were deaf, Father Bernard J. McClory conveyed the message to them in sign language. And while he didn't receive clemency, Walter Byomin got a postponement.

Bennie Collins had shot Donald Hattery, age twenty-five, after their cars collided in Toledo. Just over a year later, on December 19, 1858, he was put to death in the electric chair. "O'Neill said he reviewed Collins' case carefully and found no reason for setting aside the judgment of the courts," the *Columbus Dispatch* reported.[336] By this time, Gene had been moved to general population and was enjoying the freedom of the prison yard, where at least he could look up and see the sky, framed by rough stone walls.

Gene was lucky. He had beaten the odds. He would now be eligible for parole someday. He would now have a second chance to make a life for himself. Not so for Walter Byomin. The Cleveland cop killer's luck was about to run out. On the eve of Independence Day, July 3, 1959, he became the first person executed under the administration of Governor Michael V. DiSalle. Although the anti–death penalty governor could have granted the prisoner clemency, he declined to do so. "Last Friday night I had to sit by and see Byomin electrocuted," he told reporters. "And Saturday morning I had to ask myself what society accomplished by it."[337]

Chapter 11

IN STIR AND OUT

Do the time. Don't let the time do you.
—a jailhouse philosopher

Convicted of murder while committing a felony, Mike Dumoulin began serving a life sentence in the Ohio Penitentiary on February 7, 1958—the same day that the Brooklyn Dodgers moved to Los Angeles. In comparison to the Federal Correctional Institution at Ashland, the OP was bigger and badder. More barbaric, too. Parts of it had been built before the Civil War. And it was brimming with tough guys.

That's the thing about prison: there is always somebody tougher than you. As a Death Row inmate, Gene Peters was fairly well isolated from such concerns, but Mike—no. 104218—wasn't. Although both were inmates at the Ohio Penitentiary, the co-defendants may as well have been in two different prisons—or on two different planets. Their experiences, at least during the first year when Gene was on Death Row, would have been dramatically different. While Gene was regularly mentioned in the newspapers due to his impending execution, Mike was pretty much ignored. There was less interest in and urgency regarding his case. He had quickly become the forgotten man in the story.

After routine processing—fingerprinting, delousing, shower, haircut and so on—and a period of orientation, Mike would have been released into the general population with 4,600 other men. Owing to extreme overcrowding, he would have been assigned to a cell that contained as many as three other

Four men often lived in this two-man cell due to overcrowding. *Authors' collection.*

inmates, though intended for just two. They would have had to share a toilet, a sink and a light socket. There wasn't room for them to all stand up at once.

Three times a day, he would have been marched in a group to the mess hall for breakfast, lunch and dinner. Showers, recreation and church services generally took place once a week. Occasionally, he might have been summoned to see a psychologist or a social worker, although their caseloads were impossibly large. Otherwise, he was confined to his cell, where he and his cellmates would try to avoid getting on one another's nerves, assuming none of them was emotionally disturbed.

"We have several hundred prisoners at Ohio Penitentiary and elsewhere who could benefit from psychiatric treatment they could get at Lima," Division of Correction chief Maury Koblentz declared later that year, "if they could get in."[338]

"As an annual reminder of his crime, the court decreed that Dumoulin must hereafter spend every anniversary, July 18, in solitary confinement," the *Columbus Dispatch* reported.[339] But that lasted just three years. Prison staff had more to worry about than some whimsical order by a judge. Besides, the court must not have realized that some inmates actually beg for solitary confinement in order to escape, if only temporarily, the pressure-cooker atmosphere of being "in stir."[340] Some even went "stir crazy."

The only gang members Mike encountered were Mafioso. "You could tell who they were," he said. "They always had slick-backed hair, pointed-toe shoes. They strutted around like they was the warden."[341] Generally, they were "torpedoes"—guys hired to take the fall for higher-level gangsters. Their families were probably being supported while they were serving time for someone else's crime.

Assuming he had a job assignment, Mike would have spent maybe five or six hours a day working in some other area of the prison. Workers with dependents earned 8.5 cents per hour. Those without, 4 cents. The Ohio Penitentiary operated twenty-three different industries at the time, including the stamping of license plates. If an inmate wasn't careful, he could lose some fingers, and a few did. The woolen mill, with 426 workers, was the largest employer within the walls. But there often weren't enough jobs to keep everyone busy.

Some inmates lived in dormitories with dozens of other prisoners. Although they had less privacy, it was regarded as a step up because they had access to a common area where they could lounge around and maybe watch television and shoot pool using wooden disks instead of balls. The goal for most prisoners was to attain honor status so they could go "outside

Nearly 140 men—twice its rated capacity—were packed into this dormitory. *Authors' collection.*

the walls" to medium- or minimum-security facilities such as the London Prison Farm or Junction City, a brick manufacturing operation. Some trusties even worked at the Governor's Mansion, doing everything from lawn work to chauffeuring.

But the situation at any given time depended on the population. In April 1955, the prison population had reached an all-time high of 5,235. Although it had dropped a little over 600 men since then, it was designed for no more than 2,500. What this does is undermine all attempts at programming—education, recreation, therapy and the like. "Idleness was rampant and programs were a sham as classrooms and visiting areas had to be used for dormitories," noted John Resch, a prison historian. However, it wasn't until 1968 that a series of riots erupted that would eventually culminate in the phased closing of the Ohio Penitentiary beginning five years later.

Overcrowding was still a problem in 1958, not only at the Ohio Penitentiary but also at its sister institutions—London Prison Farm, Marion Correctional Institution and the Ohio State Reformatory at Mansfield. Under these conditions, rehabilitation was pretty much left up to the individual inmate. And the inmate's first priority was staying alive. Mike's role models could have been men such as John Morgan, although he would have been a sobering one.

Before being transferred, inmates were interviewed by the Bureau of Classification. *Authors' collection.*

The day after the Peters verdict was handed down, Morgan learned that he had been granted parole. Thirty years earlier, Jacob Rosenberg, a Cuyahoga County junk dealer, had been found dead in a house rented by Morgan. Although he insisted that he knew nothing about the man's death, Morgan was convicted of second-degree murder, largely on circumstantial evidence. On March 28, 1928, he arrived at the Ohio Penitentiary to begin serving his sentence.

Over the next three decades, Morgan was a model inmate. Now, at age ninety-four, the oldest inmate in Ohio would be leaving prison on January 23, 1958, freeing up space for new men like Gene and Mike. Morgan planned to return to "home" to Cleveland, although he had no family left to care for him.

"He claims he has enough money on the outside to take care of himself," Warden Ralph Alvis said. "I don't know about that, but I assume he has the maximum $300 in prison earnings coming to him when he is released"— that plus any money that might have been deposited in his commissary account on his behalf.[342]

When he boarded a bus that morning, Morgan was wearing a prison-made suit and was said to look fifty years younger than his age. "I don't have to work," said. "I have plenty of money."[343] Although his prison account held less than $400, including a $50 advance, he hinted there was more stashed away in New York. For the time being, he would be staying at the Salvation Army until he could find a more permanent residence.

Then there was Solly Hart, another lifer. Late in January, Warden Alvis and Hart, his longtime chauffeur, collided with the rear of a dump truck loaded with gravel. Alvis, age fifty-three, suffered facial lacerations and was blinded in the right eye. Hart, fifty-one, sustained back injuries. Although Hart, a trusty, had been the warden's driver for eighteen years, on this day Alvis was apparently behind the wheel. Once a Cleveland underworld figure, Hart "was convicted of the murder of Roy (Happy) Marino in Mahoning County in 1938."[344] He would be paroled on July 21, having served twenty years.

One month afterward, on the night of February 21, 1958, four inmates attempted to escape by going over the wall. "It was the first 'wall escape' try since Ralph Alvis became warden 10 years ago Saturday," the *Columbus Dispatch* reported.[345] There had been rumors of an escape plot for some time, so the men were being watched carefully. "They were apprehended while attempting to saw through chains holding ladders together in bundles in the prison's ladder shed."[346] The men planned to fasten the ladders together with tape in order to climb over the thirty-two-foot east wall.

It was believed that the men had outside help. As prison guards looked on, the quartet fell out of line while crossing the yard to attend a movie and entered the ladder shed. They were surprised by Deputy Warden Marion J. Koloski and a dozen armed guards.

Riots were nothing new at the Ohio Penitentiary. On March 24, 1958, a "small riot" occurred in a dormitory housing 140 "semi-trusties." It started while guards at shift change were checking to see that each prisoner was in his bed. Because there was always a light burning in the dorm, the inmates hung blankets from their bunks to serve as blinds. However, instead of just drawing back the blankets to see if the bed was occupied, one guard began yanking them down. This prompted about ten of the prisoners to start "a shouting, burning, furniture-breaking demonstration that brought scores of police and firemen to Ohio Penitentiary Monday night."[347]

In the scheme of things, it was a rather small affair. Two barrels of garbage were set ablaze, a window was broken and eight game tables were demolished. Damages amounted to less than $200. More importantly, no one was hurt, unlike in the "Easter Monday" riot and fire of 1930, which claimed 322 lives. Or the Halloween riot and fire of 1952 in which one man died and nearly $1 million in damage was done.

Every inmate does time in his own way. Some try to work the system; others fight it. Most just want the time to go by as easily as possible and frown on such disruptions as escape attempts and riots. They want to feel safe, even though they know they are living in a tinderbox.

Years later, Mike would take exception to that characterization of his role in the Coblentz tragedy. From his perspective, he and Gene were equally bad influences on each other, and he had paid the price for his actions. Sentenced to life in the Ohio Penitentiary, he resolved to make the best of it—to fit in. "I kind of liked it," he admitted, which is true of many inmates. He recalled the story of one inmate who had been there more than half a century. Immediately after he was paroled, he "went out and robbed the taxi cab driver so he could go back to prison."[348] Anyone who has worked in corrections knows of inmates who became institutionalized—they became so used to it that they couldn't function outside prison.

Given his youth, the odds were that Mike would not die in prison. According to Corrections Chief Maury Koblentz, "On the average, prisoners live longer than persons in the normal work-a-day world."[349] He attributed it to the fact that they were so closely monitored. However, a significant number of lifers did die behind bars. Over the previous ten years, seventy-seven of them died either at the Ohio Penitentiary or the London Prison Farm.

When Mike arrived at the Ohio Penitentiary, there were roughly 265 men serving life for first-degree murder, 251 for second-degree, 64 for burglary on an inhabited dwelling at night, 50 for criminal assault, 13 for being habitual criminals, 8 bank robbers and 4 kidnappers. All but those serving time for first-degree murder would be eligible for parole consideration after ten years. But most would be "flopped"—denied parole—more than once.

It was incumbent on the inmate to present himself to the parole board in the best light possible by aspiring to be a "model" prisoner. They would begin by obtaining extra privileges based on good behavior. For example, if they stayed out of trouble for six months, they were given their choice of one extra visit or writing five extra letters. But there were other programs they could avail themselves of. Forty inmates would meet every Saturday afternoon to take a fourteen-week Dale Carnegie Institute course to help prepare them to be successful when they are released.

Mike would likely have been a reader of the *Ohio Penitentiary News*, a weekly newspaper written and published by the inmates. At sixty-six years and counting, it was the second-oldest prison newspaper in the country. Warden Alvis viewed it as a morale booster. In 1958, it had a circulation of 3,900—1,200 of which were sent to subscribers outside the walls. The emphasis was on positive news, including a column on sports and medicine by Dr. Samuel H. Sheppard, no. 98860.

Sheppard, a trainer for the prison football team, the Hurricanes, also worked in the prison hospital, where he participated—as a subject—in a cancer research program sponsored by Sloan-Kettering Institute for Cancer Research. "In a quest for basic facts about immunity, volunteers at the Ohio Penitentiary had cancer cells planted beneath the skin of their arms. Their systems soon destroyed the cancer cells. Later when the same kind of cancer cells were planted again, they were destroyed even faster. The men could also throw off cells of a different type of cancer, though not quite so rapidly."[350]

Many inmates were inclined to volunteer for this and similar "controlled medical research experiments," although there sometimes was a fair amount of laxity in the control, not to mention long-term follow-up. Ninety inmates volunteered to be the test subjects for a new type of tranquilizer. "This is the kind of testing it is almost impossible to do with any other group, because the men are available at all times and can be watched for reactions," Dr. William Thomas, who was heading the project, pointed out.[351] Others participated in tularemia ("rabbit fever") tests in which they were administered a vaccine and then inhaled "living organisms of the disease."[352]

In October, some inmates provided skin grafts to a seven-year-old boy who had suffered third-degree burns over half his body. But he died anyway. While some of these inmate "guinea pigs" were truly attempting to make amends for their crimes, many were just hoping to impress the parole board. According to Mike, he was administered a test flu vaccine that put him into a coma for three days. Not surprisingly, he did not volunteer for any other medical experiments.

Thomas "Yonnie" Licavoli, age fifty-four, was a Toledo mobster who led "members of the old Purple Gang."[353] A contemporary of Al Capone's, Licavoli was sent to the Ohio Penitentiary for a gangland slaying of four people and had been there twenty-four years. In November 1958, Warden Ralph W. Alvis ordered Licavoli returned from the Hocking Honor Camp near Logan when the *Columbus Dispatch* published a story claiming that he was receiving special privileges. While the warden was inclined not to believe it, he did order an investigation.

Some of the accusations included unlimited visitors on non-visiting days—including Teamsters boss James Hoffa, although this was denied—

Like many gangsters, "Yonnie" Liccavoli still wielded power behind bars. *From the* Columbus Citizen, *Scripps-Howard Newspaper/Grandview Heights Public Library/ Photohio.org.*

special meals served apart from the other prisoners, uncensored mail, non-regulation clothing (e.g., sun-tan pants, a polo shirt and a sweater), use of the camp telephone, access to a small cabin (which he purportedly purchased from another inmate for forty dollars) for him and his visitors and freedom to visit nearby communities.

Alvis claimed that the accusations were "grossly exaggerated," although he then seemed to confirm some of them were true ("uninspected packages could not contain narcotics and liquor" because the "guards would spot anyone using liquor or narcotics").[354]

Licavoli had been in the prison camp for three years, but his prison record was far from spotless. In 1935, the year after Licavoli arrived, Attorney General John W. Bricker investigated allegations and special treatment. These led to the ouster of Warden Preston E. Thomas.[355] "Licavoli had a little house—it isn't there any more—right in the prison grounds," one investigator recalled, "and he had absolute say about who lived there with him. He had it for his castle, had pretty well taken things over. He had

Christmas dinner cooked outside at a restaurant and sent down to him at the prison."[356]

Four years later, Licavoli "was cited as the ringleader in a banking and gambling scheme within the pen walls. The probe produced evidence of liquor and narcotics being brought inside the penitentiary."[357] This investigation lead to the removal of Warden James C. Woodard. Under Acting Warden William F. Amrine, Licavoli allegedly did much the same thing, but penitentiary records were burned to cover it up.

In the end, the Ohio State Highway Patrol confirmed that Licavoli had received special privileges. It "found a general laxity in operations at the camp," and Lieutenant Thomas Crowe of Logan, the officer in charge, was forced to resign.[358] He had purportedly received a few gifts from the gangster's friend: nine bottles of whiskey, a footstool and a magazine rack. He had also had attended Licavoli's daughter's wedding in Detroit.

During Licavoli's time at Hocking Honor Camp, his family purchased venetian blinds and draperies for the camp office, a television, a pool table, a cash register and an adding machine, asphalt tile for the dining room and a swing set for use by children on visiting day. He would be paroled in 1972 after thirty-eight years.

Looking back, Mike said that he knew both Sheppard and Licavoli, as well as "lots of guys from Wooster and Millersburg."[359] Eventually, he was entrusted with making job assignments to all newly arriving inmates (there were numerous instances of guards treating lifers like they were junior prison staff). However, for the most part, his time in pen proved to be uneventful. "I had no problems at all" he said.[360]

On March 31, 1965, seven years after he arrived at the prison, Mike was transferred to Marion Correctional Institution, Marion, Ohio. MCI was classified as a minimum- to medium-security facility. Superintendent Lamoyne A. Greene was in charge. He was a holdover from when the facility was the Marion Training School, a sister institution of the Ohio State Reformatory for younger and less dangerous offenders. It had been created from the former administrative buildings of the wartime Scioto Ordnance Plant.

Opened in 1955, MCI was still considered a modern complex a decade later. Instead of a wall, it was surrounded by a sixteen-foot chain-link fence, topped with barbed wire and a separate ten-foot fence inside that, also sporting barbed wire. In 1966, it held 1,400 inmates; it was built to house 1,500.

Roughly 40 percent of the population at MCI was African American, about the same percentage as other Ohio institutions. However, unlike the Ohio Penitentiary, the inmates were not racially segregated. Mike felt that this

Corrections Chief Maury Koblentz and Superintendent Lamoyne Greene inspect a Marion cellblock. *Authors' collection.*

reduced tension and violence. "Everyone got along," he said.[361] It also operated a furniture factory, a garment factory and a sheet metal shop. Inmates raised beef, chicken, pork and a variety of vegetables on its farm, so the food was considered better than at most other prisons.

During his tenure at Marion, Mike enrolled in the stationary engineer program and was trained to be a boiler operator. This was a very good trade at the time and provided him with the necessary skills to land a good job upon his release.

On May 15, 1968, Gene joined his co-defendant at the MCI. One year earlier, his father, Myron, had passed away in 1967 at the age of fifty-one. It is highly unlikely that

Don King was once an inmate at Marion Correctional Institution. *Gage Skidmore, Wikimedia Commons.*

he attended the funeral. His mother, Estella, then remarried and moved to Washington.

Don King, perhaps Marion Correctional Institution's most famous "graduate," was already there when Gene arrived. Inmate no. 125734, King had gotten into a fight over money with Sam Garrett, one of his employees. During their altercation, Garrett's head struck the pavement, and he eventually died. Although King claimed self-defense—as he had when he killed another man, Hillary Brown, in 1954—this time he was convicted of manslaughter. He would serve four years.

"King used his time in prison to give himself the education that he had earlier chosen to bypass. For four years he immersed himself in classic literature and philosophy. When he was released on parole in 1971, King was, as he told a *TV Guide* interviewer in 1980, 'armed and dangerous. Armed with wisdom and knowledge.'"[362] In 1977, he returned to MCI, this time as a world-famous fight promoter, to stage a nationally televised program live from within the prison. Accompanying him was announcer Howard Cosell and former heavyweight champion Joe Louis.

On August 28, 1972, Mike's sentence was commuted to second-degree murder, making him eligible for parole. He was released from the Marion Correctional Institution on October 5, 1972, some seven and a half years after he was transferred there from the Ohio Penitentiary. He had served a total of fourteen years, seven months and twenty-nine days. Richard

Nixon—Eisenhower's former vice president—was now president, and the radio was playing "Baby, Don't Get Hooked on Me" by Mac Davis. Mike was wearing a prison-made suit that marked him as an ex-con to those in the know.

Since Gene and Mike entered the correctional system, Ohio's prison population had dropped by one-third. Dr. Bennett J. Cooper, director of the Ohio Department of Rehabilitation and Corrections, attributed the decrease to "increased parole rates and improved community treatment programs…despite the increase in commitments by the courts."[363] Ready or not, nearly 70 percent of the six thousand inmates eligible for parole each year were being set free. Mike returned to Holmes County, followed shortly by Gene, where they were under the supervision of the Canton District Parole Office for the next five years. Despite all they had been through, they remained friends.

Chapter 12

KITH AND KIN

We know what we are, but know not what we may be.
—William Shakespeare[364]

Gene Peters admitted killing one man and wounding another. Mike Dumoulin allegedly assaulted a young mother and her infant daughter. Both men were guilty of robbery, auto theft, evading arrest and who knows what else. They were even accused, briefly, of conspiring to kill a county sheriff.

Gene was sent to the Ohio Penitentiary to die and Mike to live out his life behind bars. Neither pronouncement would come to pass. Both would eventually walk out the prison gates as free men. Both would have the larger part of their lives ahead of them.

Make no mistake about it, Gene and Mike were bad men when they went to prison—or, at the very least, men behaving badly. Given their prior records, there was little reason to believe either one was a likely candidate for reform. And yet…the Amish and their Mennonite brethren were willing—even eager—to forgive them. To paraphrase Robert Schenck, the grandfather of one of the murdered Amish girls at Nickel Mines: "We must not think evil of [these men]."[365] Such judgments are left to God.

Not long after Gene's sentence was commuted, two ministers visited him in prison. He told them he was deeply appreciative of the many letters of prayers and forgiveness he had received, including at least one from Dora Coblentz, the widow of the man he had slain. He also said he had become a Christian.

New members of an Alcoholics Anonymous class held at the prison. *Authors' collection.*

The following July, an article in the *Gospel Herald*, a Mennonite magazine, provided an update:

> *Cleo Eugene Peters, serving a life sentence in the Ohio State Penitentiary, Columbus, Ohio, is an active student in* The Mennonite Hour *correspondence course on "God's Great Salvation." Peters was convicted of the murder of Paul Coblentz, an Amish young man, and sentenced to the electric chair. Eight hours before he was to go to the death chamber he was pardoned by the governor of Ohio at the intercession of Amish people. He found peace with the Lord a few weeks before he was to die. He is now doing good work on his correspondence course, in which he was enrolled by brethren interested in his spiritual welfare.*[366]

"The whole event had a marked impact on the Holmes County Amish," Stephen Russell related. "'God has been speaking to many of us Amish people through this act,' several church leaders wrote to Peters. 'We believe that God allowed this, especially to call us back to Him in the work of winning souls to His kingdom.'"[367]

This "ministry of reconciliation" extended to Mike as well. He said that the Amish and Mennonites wrote letters and sent him literature too. But they did not visit him, and he never heard from any member of the Coblentz family. This apparent disparity in treatment was likely due to the fact Mike did not have a death sentence hanging over his head.

Delegates to the 1963 biennial conference of Mennonites meeting in Iowa were urged to consider "a statement that would condemn states that maintain the death penalty, saying such states…'arguably usurp the role of God himself.'"[368] The statement pointed out that when Peters was sentenced to die, "friends and neighbors of the slain man signed petitions requesting a commutations of the sentence. The commutation was granted."[369]

The following year, former Ohio governor Michael V. DiSalle wrote, "There was a belief in the community that Dumoulin was more or less the leader" in the Coblentz slaying.[370] So, in commuting Gene's death sentence, Governor O'Neill, at least in part, relied on the principle of "comparative justice [as] the basis for his action when he noted that: 'Under the law they were equally guilty.'"[371]

Twenty years after Paul's murder, the Amish and Mennonite response to the crime remained a topic of discussion. At a series of hearings before the U.S. House of Representatives Subcommittee on Criminal Justice in 1978, Delton Franz of the Mennonite Central Committee recalled, "There are numerous instances in which the family and friends of the victims, and sometimes the larger community, have asked that revenge not be taken and that help be sought to rehabilitate the defendant. Such, at least, was the response of the Coblentz family, their fellow church and community members."[372]

A decade later, the U.S. Congress once again cited the case during hearings on the death penalty:

> When Cleo Eugene Peters was sentenced to die for his murder of Paul Coblenz…the friends and neighbors of the murdered man signed petitions requesting a commutation of the sentence.…In the meantime they carried on a ministry of reconciliation, through visitation of the condemned man in prison and manifestations of friendship to his family, and with a least some resulting evidence of personal rehabilitation.[373]

Although it was tragic, Paul had not died for nothing. The response of the Amish and Mennonite community to his murder would become one of the most enduring arguments against capital punishment. But was their underlying hope for Gene and Mike's redemption justified?

Prior to being paroled, inmates at Marion received a weeklong "indoctrination." *Authors' collection.*

Three weeks after he walked out of prison, Mike married Evelyn Roberta Moyer. Born in 1937, in Quakertown, Pennsylvania, "Robbie," as Mike called her, was the daughter of Alvin Godshall Moyer and Mabel Ruth Hunsberger. According to John Miller, Alvin was "a pleasant individual who

Gene Peters was born in picturesque Muscatine, Iowa. *Wikimedia Commons*.

in the 1940s had an egg route through the Holmes County area."[374] He would pass away less than a year after Robbie's marriage to Mike.

While Mike was sitting in the Holmes County Jail awaiting trial for murder, Robbie was embarking on the first of several marriages. Following graduation from Millersburg High School and the Gale Institute Airlines School in Minneapolis, she met and married Alvin Ronald Millichamp. She was twenty-one. The newlyweds made their home in Denton, Texas, where Alvin was attending college.

In January 1958, one month before Mike would go on trial, the Millichamps returned to Ohio, where they were feted at a dinner party in Millersburg hosted by Robbie's parents. Among the other guests were Mr. and Mrs. Darryl Weiss and Mr. and Mrs. Jack Montieth. Darryl, the son of Sheriff Harry Weiss, was married to Robbie's sister, Claire, and had assisted in Mike's arrest. Jack was married to Robbie's sister Grace.

However, Robbie's marriage was a troubled one, and by September, she had filed for divorce. She then moved back to Millersburg, where she landed a job as a supervisor at the Ohio Central Telephone Company.

The following summer, Robbie entered into her second marriage on July 26, 1959, this time to Fred A. Badertscher, a manager of the Killbuck Drilling Company. It was the first wedding performed in the new St. John's United Church of Christ in Millersburg, where her father served as superintendent of the Sunday school.

At some point, the Badertschers divorced as well. Robbie then married Wayne E. Buehler, by whom she had one child. Wayne was president of Buehler Food Markets Inc., a local grocery chain based in Wooster. They remained married for at least six years. They were divorced, however, by the time of Wayne's death on January 12, 1972. He had suffered a heart attack and struck a utility pole while driving his car.

Mike related that he had known Robbie since they were about thirteen years old, and she had begun writing him while he was in prison. When they married, they were both thirty-five. It was his first marriage. Their only child was born in 1974 while they were living in Smithville.

In addition to being "a homemaker," Robbie held a private pilot's license, belonged to an organization of female pilots and, according to Mike, won a number of trophies racing Karmann Ghia automobiles at tracks in New York. Robbie was also active in the Order of the Eastern Star. They both attended the local Baptist church.

Mike Dumoulin knew about the Amish from growing up in Wayne County. *Cleveland Public Library/Photograph Collection.*

On October 6, 1977, five years after he walked out of the Marion Correctional Institution, Mike was released from parole. "I learned a lot in prison," Mike recalled. "I did a lot of studying and minding my own business."[375] The Dumoulins were living in Wooster, and Mike was working as a stationary engineer at the Orville Municipal Electrical Plant. It was a trade he had learned while at Marion. In his free time, he hunted, canoed and collected Indian relics as a member of the Ohio Archaeological Society.

After eleven years, Mike quit his job at the electrical plant, weary of working swing shifts. He also said that many of his co-workers were using drugs on the job. So he began working as an "Amish taxi cab" driver—one of a number of non-Amish persons who made a living chauffeuring Amish people in motorized vehicles. Eventually, he went to work at D.C. Curry Lumber in Wooster, transporting crews of Amish carpenters to various job sites, where he worked beside them building houses and other structures.

Meanwhile, Robbie operated Westwood Connection, an alternative music shop near the College of Wooster Campus. Not only did she sell records, tapes, CDs, posters, T-shirts and tapestries, but she also booked bands. Sadly, the Dumoulins' seventeen-year marriage came to an end on March 11, 1990, when Robbie succumbed to brain cancer at the age of fifty-three. She died in the arms of her nurse, a woman named "Peg" (Margaret) whom Mike described as an "Okie," a native of Oklahoma.[376] Mike subsequently married Peg, and the couple moved to Idabell, Oklahoma.

Before Mike's mother, Emma, passed away in Wooster in 1994, she had placed his father, George, in a rest home. "He wanted out of there bad," Mike said.[377] So they took him along with them and arranged for Gene and his wife, Dawn, who were living just south in Broken Bow, Oklahoma, to take care of him. Dropping in to visit one evening, Mike found that his father had been left alone with Dawn's two sons, ages seven and nine. Mike immediately fired Gene and took his father home with him. George Dumoulin died in Oklahoma in 1997 at the age of eighty-seven.

After leaving Ohio, Mike "raised longhorn steers."[378] He also worked as a carpenter in an automobile machine shop and for Tyson chicken. "I don't shrink from work," he asserted.[379] But a decade or so later, Mike and Peg divorced. She was twenty-three years younger than he, and the age difference had begun to drive a wedge between them. According to Mike, "She started going back to school and she became an EMT. And she wanted me to become an EMT. I don't really like picking bodies off the highway. And she really loved it. So I told her, well, this is the end of the road."[380]

Single again, Mike moved to Louisiana, bought a houseboat and lived in the swamps for five years. "The fishing was fantastic," Mike recalled.[381] He also lived with his daughter in Ohio for a few years, but the snow soon drove him down to Arkansas. Now, at the age of eighty-three, Mike lives in the mountains and spends most days at his camper fishing or hunting for crystals. He claims that he has not gotten into any more trouble since his release from prison, and nothing has come to light to suggest otherwise.

Looking back over his life, Mike firmly believes that he would not have turned to religion if it hadn't been for his involvement in the slaying of Paul Coblentz. "I didn't think about it back then," he said.[382] However, once in prison, he "decided to walk the straight path" in an effort to redeem himself.[383] Although he never had any further contact with the Coblentz family, he asserts, "I pray for Paul's family all the time."[384]

Originally a Baptist, Mike later became a "Sabbath-keeper"—an offshoot of the Seventh-day Adventists—when he moved to Louisiana. He remains active in the church to this day, spending every Saturday in a beautiful chapel deep in the forests of "God's Country," as the locals call it.

The obituary of Michael George Dumoulin has yet to be written. He has outlived Paul Coblentz by more than three score years, and he accepts responsibility for his part in that. The Amish would likely be pleased to know that he is, apparently, a religious man. Although they believe their own faith is the true one, they tend to be respectful and accepting of other religions because they do not presume to know God's will—or Mike's heart.

Gene Peters was released from prison on March 29, 1973, even as the last remaining American combat troops were being pulled out of Vietnam. He had been at MCI a little over four years and ten months. Like his co-defendant, he had been granted clemency, and his sentence was reduced from first- to second-degree murder. Gene had served a total of fifteen years, three months and seventeen days of a "life" sentence. During this period, the Ohio Parole Board was hearing about five hundred to six hundred cases per month. Because it was so overtaxed, the six-person board (down one member due to a resignation) was using two-member panels to hear most cases.

Later that year, William McKee, the Richland County prosecutor, objected to the practice of granting paroles to convicted felons before they had served their minimum sentences. McKee charged that "the Adult Parole Authority has been releasing convicts on a reduced schedule 'which they themselves made up—ignoring the schedule determined by the legislature and incorporated in Ohio law.'"[385] In this case, a man who was originally sentenced to death was now walking the streets.

A special bus transported inmates from one institution to another. *Authors' collection.*

Mike Dumoulin, who had gotten out five months before, assisted Gene in getting settled in the area. Both were under the authority of the Canton district parole office. By the next year, the Canton district office was experiencing a staff shortage, limiting its ability to effectively monitor and manage parolees. But neither of them appear to have required much management.

Robbie thought highly enough of Gene that she introduced him to her sister, Grace. According to Mike, Grace wrote to Gene while he was in prison and visited him on several occasions. They were subsequently married on October 24, 1975, in Stark County, Ohio. Gene was thirty-seven and living in North Canton, and Grace was forty-five.

Grace was born in 1930 in Silverdale, Pennsylvania, to Alvin and Mabel Moyer. Given her age, it is not surprising that Grace, like Robbie, had been married previously. In 1953, at the age of twenty-three, she wed John Elmer "Jack" Montieth (or "Monteith") and settled in Orrville, where he worked as a chemist. They had at least two children. However, that was not enough to keep them together.

Grace Montieth, age thirty-four, took out a marriage license with Joseph Eugene Unger, an air force officer from Columbus, in 1964, but it does not appear that they actually followed through. Three years later, Mrs. Grace Monteith was director of the St. John's United Church of Christ junior choir.

In 1969, Grace, now thirty-nine and employed as a medical assistant, married Harold Wheaton, forty-six, an assistant postmaster. A graduate of Capital University, Harold was a member of the church choir for many years. During their short-lived marriage, Grace gave presentations on the "Life and Customs of the Navaho Indians," based on her personal observations. She was also elected treasurer of the Kno-Ho-Co (Knox, Holmes and Coshocton Counties) Community Action Commission.

After they were wed, Gene and Grace settled down in Grace's residence, a nice brick house in Massillon, Ohio. Mike remembered that Gene "was a cook and he worked for a transfer…a moving company."[386] But he does not know if he was steadily employed.

On March 29, 1978, Gene was released from parole. What should have been a happy time, however, was cut short by Grace's death eight months later. They had been married for three years. Although Gene continued to live in the Massillon area, Mike recalled that they did not see each other very often. Their friendship was a one-sided affair, with Mike helping him out on occasion and Gene seldom reciprocating.

Twelve years later, on January 17, 1990, Gene married Dawn Marie Gerst in Wooster, Ohio. He had met her in Illinois, Mike said. Dawn was quite a bit younger, having been born in 1963 in Monmouth, Illinois, while Gene was still a prisoner at the Ohio Penitentiary. She had previously been married to Frederick Vessie Blake and Leslie Robert Blackman and had a son by each. They apparently divorced as well, for she remarried in 2005.

According to Mike, Gene had an ongoing problem with alcohol that ultimately contributed to his death. "He killed himself with his diet and a case of beer every day," he related.[387] Perhaps that was his way of dealing with the guilt he felt for taking a man's life. They continued to keep in touch over the years and even lived near each other in Oklahoma. However, Mike lost contact with him when he left Oklahoma and was living in Louisiana when Gene died. When he last saw him, Gene was in bad shape due to "an enlarged heart."[388]

Little is known of Gene's life from that point until his death at 6:10 p.m. on August 3, 2015, at his home in Monmouth, Illinois, at the age of seventy-seven. According to his obituary, "He enjoyed gardening, especially rhubarb, reading and a good intellectual debate. He was a very generous person who on many occasions opened his home to friends and family."[389]

For a time, Gene had worked as a cook at Sharon's Bar & Grill in Monmouth, but there was no other mention of how he had made a living over the years. Three sons were listed as survivors—two of these were apparently the sons Dawn brought to their marriage. Gene was cremated, and his remains were buried at Eliza Creek Cemetery, Mercer County, Illinois.

As far as can be determined, Gene seemingly turned his life around, too, or at least stayed out of additional trouble. Although much was made of the fact that Gene had become a Christian while in prison, Mike was unaware of it. "As far as I knew, he never went to church," Mike said.[390] Of course, this does not mean it wasn't true, but perhaps it was wishful thinking on the part of those who were determined to save not only his life but also his soul.

If not the biggest case of Sheriff Harry Weiss's career, the murder of Paul Coblentz was the most unusual—and not just because the victim was Amish. In a plot twist worthy of a television soap opera, Harry would later find himself "welcoming" both Mike Dumoulin and Gene Peters into his extended family.

Darryl, Harry's son, had married Theda Claire Moyer, the eldest of Alvin and Mabel Moyer's five daughters, in 1941. Born in 1921, Claire had graduated from high school in Souderton, Pennsylvania, just prior to her family's relocation to Ohio, where her father entered the egg business. From that point, the two families were intertwined—familially, socially and spiritually as well. They all attended St. John's Church.

Then, in 1957, Sheriff Weiss and his son traveled to Illinois to take custody of the two men who would later be convicted of the murder—

Peters and Dumoulin. Their first impressions of the two young men could not have been good.

Three years later, Sheriff Weiss lost his bid for reelection to Republican James Taylor. Only a year earlier, Harry was regaling the members of the Sugarcreek Rotary Club with a detailed account of the Coblentz murder and the apprehension of the killers. But somehow his celebrity hadn't translated into votes. He was replaced by one of the youngest sheriffs in the state.

Following the election, Harry was given a citation by the Buckeye Sheriffs Association in recognition of his work in solving the murder of Harvey Harpster the year before. Harpster had been found shot to death in his cottage near Lakeville. Although Harry was also awarded a life membership in the sheriffs association, once again he was out of a job. But in 1960, he bounced back, unseating Taylor in a three-way race for the office.

Seven years after that, Sheriff Weiss resigned. Although no reason was given, it was generally known when he was reelected to his sixth term that he needed only two more years to reach retirement age. During his tenure, he had enjoyed an especially good relationship with the Amish citizens of Holmes County.[391] His son, Darryl, replaced him.

For the next ten years, until 1977, Darryl served as sheriff of Holmes County. Like his father, he also spoke German and Pennsylvania German. It was during that time that Mike and Gene married his sisters-in-law. According to Mike, the Weiss family always "treated us real good. No tension at all."[392] However, Bob Gerber, son of Evelyn Weiss and grandson of Harry Weiss, told his daughter, Amy Doerfler, that "the ladies never brought their husbands around the family."[393] Neither did he ever hear any mention of their crime. According to Mike, the many Amish with whom he worked on a daily basis never discussed it, either, although the story remains alive in the community to this day.

After he lost a bid for reelection, Darryl was hired as a patrolman in Millersburg. Two years later, he became the Millersburg chief of police, an office he held for the next eleven years. Fortunately, he never again had to arrest his brothers-in-law.

Chapter 13

THE QUIET IN THE LAND

For they speak not peace: but they devise deceitful matters
against them that are quiet in the land.
—Book of Psalms 35:20[394]

The impact of Paul's death on Dora must have been devastating. Not
only did she lose her husband, but her home, her financial well-being
and her status as a wife as well. One moment she knew who she was, the
next she didn't. She was adrift in uncharted waters. "Across the spectrum
of Amish life," anthropologist Karen Johnson-Weiner has written, "Amish
women hope to marry and raise families within the church."[395] That is the
default role. That is what they spend their adolescence preparing for. That
is God's plan.

The Amish are a family-oriented society. The husband manages the farm
(or, nowadays, business), the wife manages the home and the children are in
training to assume the roles of husband and wife when they have families
of their own. Chores are gender segregated. Women clean, cook, sew and
perform the other duties traditionally considered "women's work."

A single Amish woman who has never married or is widow, however,
has no particular role. In social situations, they have little in common
with married women and "must constantly shy away from men to avoid
embarrassment and gossip."[396] However, "Sexual harassment of a single
woman by a married man has rarely occurred," researcher Duchang Cong
has reported. "Indeed, the nunlike status of single women serves to prevent
them from being forced into unpleasant situations."[397]

Dora was not only a widow—she was a young widow. "In a situation like that," Abraham Hochstetler observed, "typically the community would take care of her. She wouldn't hold any type of special position, but everyone would feel the sense of community to help take care of her and her children."[398] Thanks to her Amish community, Dora would have been, in some ways, much better off than her English counterpart who lacked a church safety net.

As a rule, whenever there is a death, the Amish will provide some level of support—emotional and, possibly, financial—to those impacted for at least a year. But, in reality, how much help could Dora have expected and from whom?

The Amish are known for their generosity in the face of tragedy, even shown toward people outside of their insular community. When five Amish girls were gunned down in a Pennsylvania schoolhouse, money poured in from around the world. One year later, the Nickel Mines Accountability Committee, which was set up to handle the donations, found itself with $4.3 million. These funds were dispersed to the Amish families who lost children and to those of five other girls who were wounded, as well as to Marie Roberts, the widow of Charles Carl Roberts, the gunman. This was in recognition of the fact that she had three children of her own to raise alone.

Old Order Amish remain a familiar sight in a number of Ohio towns. *Library of Congress.*

It is not unusual for Amish people to send checks to other Amish people they don't know after reading about some misfortune or another in *The Budget*, an Amish newspaper. Based in Sugarcreek, Ohio, *The Budget* has a national—even international—reach. However, Dora would have received nowhere near the level of support that many do because her need wouldn't have been as great as some others. After all, she had only one child to support and a family to return to, including siblings and two living parents, John E. Yoder and Mary Ann Miller.

However, at the time of Paul's death, the Millers were both in their mid-sixties. They were at an age when they were likely thinking about retirement, if they hadn't already done so. When Dora moved back in with them, it wasn't the same home she had left less than three years before and her place in it wouldn't have been the same either. Undoubtedly, her return to their household, along with her daughter, Esther, forced them to modify their plans.

The Yoder family consisted of nine children—four sons and five daughters—ranging in age from seventeen to forty. Presumably, all but Dora's younger brother, Eli, age twenty-one, and younger sister, Ella, seventeen, would have moved out before she moved back in. Three months later, Eli married Susan J. Hershberger on October 15, 1957. Usually, he would have been in line to take over the family farm. But if he had any plans to occupy the big house—assuming they had two houses—they would have likely been deferred to accommodate the needs of his parents, two sisters and a niece. That is, unless Dora found some place else to live.

It is possible that Ella J., Dora's youngest sister, also continued to live in her parents' house for nearly ten more years. She does not appear to have married until 1966. She was twenty-seven and working as a domestic at the time, and her husband, Noah E. Yoder, was nineteen and working as a farmer.

Typically, an Amish family will observe a yearlong period of mourning. During that time, Dora would have dressed in black whenever she was in public. This serves as a reminder of her bereavement to others in the community so they can respond accordingly.

More than fifteen years after Paul's death, Naomi Huyard, an Amish woman, was slain in Lancaster County, Pennsylvania. Naomi's niece, Emma King, later recalled that the family had company every day and evening for three months. This was not unusual for an Amish family under the circumstances, and it was likely that Dora experienced a similar year's worth of Sunday visits. One of the visitors to Emma's family was Dora, who had heard about their tragedy. Although she had remarried by then, she apparently still felt a need to share her experience. However, Emma could not bring herself to meet with her. "I was not sure that I would be able to handle hearing about one more tragedy," she wrote.[399]

Tragedies, big and small, are not unknown to the Amish. John C. Miller, Dora's cousin, published *Tragedies Along County Road 235*, a chronicle of thirty or so such incidents that occurred on a 5.4-mile stretch of road that wound past the Coblentz farm. However, most of them were automobile or farm accidents. Paul's death was the only murder.

Dora's mother was no stranger to heartbreak. On March 2, 1950, just three months after her own mother passed away, her brother, Levi N. Miller, was burned to death when an oil stove exploded. He "had been in poor mental health for a number of years" and was trapped in his home, which was completely consumed by the fire.[400]

More than a half century later, Dora wrote about her uncle Levi. He was born in 1897 and fell victim to "brain fever"—possibly meningitis or encephalitis—in his childhood. This reduced his mental capacity to the point where "he became just like a wild animal, naked and vicious."[401] Out of compassion, Dora's parents offered to take him in. They built a cottage for him and his mother next to their own house, but his mother soon left to live with another of her children, leaving Levi in the Yoders' care.

Although no one could really control Levi, who was surprisingly strong, he seemed to respond to Dora better than the others. But even she had to hold him at bay with a stick to keep him from hitting her. Eventually, they had to put bars on the windows and a steel door on the little house to keep him from escaping at night and harming himself. On one occasion, he severely cut his face when he walked into a hay mower cutter bar, and on another he had nearly frozen to death.

By the time of the fire, Levi was fifty-two years old, blind and deaf. An oil heating stove was kept in the cottage outside his room where he couldn't reach it. But on a windy March day the stove had blown over, setting the building ablaze. Dora's mother, "who had visited him only a half hour before the fire, discovered the blaze when she took lunch to the cottage home."[402] Although she tried to rescue him, the flames drove her back. "They think he died from the smoke inhalation, but he was also burned rather badly," Dora recalled.[403] Dora's mother later told John Miller that it was "sad that they couldn't view him wearing a suit [at the funeral], as they hadn't been able to keep clothes on him when he was alive."[404]

Six years after Paul's death, tragedy struck the family once again. On June 10, 1963, Andrew D. Troyer, age forty, of Lakeview, and his son, Henry A., fifteen, "were working on a hay fork in a neighbor's barn when the equipment broke and both fell [twenty-five feet] to the floor."[405] Andrew sustained a fractured pelvis, broken arm and internal injuries. He died seventeen days later. His son's injuries were not as serious.

Andrew was the husband of Clara J. Yoder, Dora's older sister. They were married on February 18, 1943. He was survived by his widow, three daughters and six sons. The eldest child, a daughter, was nineteen. Consequently, all of Andrew and Clara's children were probably still living at home.

On January 19, 1972, tragedy struck the Yoder family yet again. Henry J. Yoder, Dora's eldest brother, hanged himself at his home in Fountain Nook. He was fifty-five. "Surviving are his parents, Mr. and Mrs. John E. Yoder of RD 2, Fredericksburg; his widow, Edna; [and] five children."[406]

Although Wayne County coroner Dr. Donald Nofziger ruled that the cause of Henry's death was suicide, his finding was immediately disputed. As noted in the *Amish Paradox*, "Yoder's death certificate listed 'apoplexy' (stroke) as the principal cause…and…a letter was written by Old Order deacon John Y. Schlabach and signed by John E. Yoder as a rebuttal to the persistent suicide rumors."[407] Once more, the church community would have been expected to provide support.

When compared to the hardships of Clara and her nine children or Edna and her five, Dora and her one daughter would have required far fewer resources, and it is likely that she relied primarily on her immediate family. While there is no way of knowing exactly what she went through in the years that followed, it is reasonable to assume that she spent the next thirteen living with her parents or one of her siblings. Or she could have even moved out on her own. But research has shown that even those who live independently still maintain close relationship with their families, sometimes occupying a small house on the edge of their parents' or siblings' property.

Both single Amish men and women benefit from some flexibility when it comes to interpretation of the *Ordnung*, allowing them to work outside the home. For example, single woman often become teachers, waitresses or domestics, while the single men take jobs in nearby factories or on construction crews. Historically, single women found domestic work or as caregivers in "English" homes. Dora may well have been hired to care for children, perform housework or look after the elderly in nearby Fredericksburg. At least one of her sisters had done so. Nowadays, she would be more inclined to obtain factory work or take a job in a non-Amish business.

"Single women…maintain close relationships with their siblings, especially married sisters," according to Cong. "They tend to form strong ties with their nephews and nieces. In many cases, nephews and nieces take care of their single aunts when the latter become old and sick."[408]

That was what Emma King witnessed. "Growing up with two single aunts and seeing their lifestyle appealed to us girls so much that it instilled in our minds that it would be a very nice way to live."[409] However, one of the aunts told them they would surely become lonely when they grew older. "She practically lived for her nieces and nephews which made her a special pet to all of them," Emma related.[410] She also wrote many letters, often visited the sick and assisted with funerals. According to Emma, Dora could have expected visits from sympathetic family and friends on the anniversary of Paul's death.

In a study of bereavement and mortality, it was found that "remarriage plays an important role in improving the survival rate of men and women in the Amish population."[411] The researchers had hypothesized that the loss of a spouse would be partially mitigated among the Amish because of the unusually supportive social structure. But this did not appear to be the case.

If Amish women have aged out of the customary boy-girl activities such as the Sunday night sing, they have few other opportunities to socialize with the opposite sex. Single women are already at a disadvantage because there are more of them than there are single Amish men, particularly as they grow older. "Among the Amish, single women outnumber single men, in part because a higher percentage of young men than women choose not to be baptized, creating a 'marriage squeeze.'"[412] In addition, there are more single Amish women because more Amish men die earlier, often due to farm accidents. It is not unusual for these "single sisters" to feel left out of the nuclear family, which is the focus of church and school activities.

Those who are not selected for marriage likely feel that it is either because they are not sufficiently attractive or sufficiently forward. And if they turn to the Bible for solace, they are hard pressed to find it. Because of the unique position of these "single sisters," a group called the Association of Unmarried Amish Women sponsor an annual reunion that encompasses several settlements. The formation of this group came long after Dora's time, however. As an unmarried Old Order woman told researchers, "Amish women are content because they deny their feelings. They wear a lot of masks."[413]

Amish women who are not married or engaged by their middle twenties likely won't ever be. But most continue to hold out hope even as they enter middle age. Add in those who are widowed and their numbers are significant. There is always the chance that they might find an Amish widower who is seeking a companion. Because single women generally spend more time caring for their parents than their married siblings, Amish parents often try to make special provisions for their single daughters, helping them to start small businesses or arranging for housing. Unmarried Amish women often work as teachers, nursing home attendants, restaurant workers or for other family members—in the case of Katie Coblentz, as a poultry dresser.

Ironically, Cong has noted, "They tend to be the most educated, and often play essential intellectual roles. They fill important occupations slots, such as teachers, health care providers, and business managers. Many act as financiers for family and friends."[414]

While it is possible that Dora did not want to remarry right away, she would have been under pressure to do so simply because the role of an Amish woman is to be a wife, mother and homemaker. Without a husband and a home of her own, she would have seemed incomplete as an adult woman in her community and, perhaps, socially stunted. But the prospects for remarriage were slim. Because there are many more widows than widowers, Amish men are more apt to remarry.[415]

Researcher Gayle Livecchia had identified two types of remarriage: "family formation marriage" and "companion marriage."[416] Obviously, the former requires that the woman be of child-bearing age, which Dora was at the time of her husband's death. The latter generally involves an "old girl" who is close to the man in age but no longer can bear children. As the term implies, it is a remarriage built on a desire for companionship.

When Dora finally remarried thirteen years after her husband's death, it could have been for either or both reasons. She was thirty-nine when she and a forty-one-year-old widowed farmer from Apple Creek took out a marriage license in late 1970. He was also Old Order Amish. Overnight, Dora became stepmother to three sons and a daughter, while Esther, an only child, found herself with four stepsiblings.

Although Mose and Susie Coblentz moved to Sarasota, Florida, immediately following their son's death, they did not remain there long. Returning to Ohio in March, they purchased a twenty-acre farm from Mr. and Mrs. Isaac Weaver east of Mount Hope near Winesburg. Their daughter, Katie, who was twenty-one when her brother was slain, married a Fredericksburg farmer in October 1959. A few years later, the Coblentzes moved back to their original farm. Mose died there seven years later on December 6, 1977, at the age of seventy-five. He had been born in Holmes County on January 7, 1902. Susie followed on March 4, 1995. She was

The Coblentz farm as seen from the Saltcreek Township House. *Author photo.*

ninety-one, having been born on February 8, 1904. Both are buried at a family cemetery in Ohio.

Old Order Amish by birth, Ira Wagler turned his back on his heritage and chose not to join the church. Consequently, he has lived as both Amish and "English." In his memoir, *Growing Up Amish*, he wrote, "Even among the Amish, other Amish seem odd."[417]

The Amish as a group value privacy and discretion. The very basis of their faith and culture is built on separation—standing apart from the non-Amish world. This tends to foster an air of mystery about them that is irresistible to tourists. And if Amish men seem mysterious, Amish women, especially young girls, are even more so—much as they are in the larger society. At times, they even seem invisible.

Yet for all their invisibility—a byproduct of living in male-dominated families—many Amish women and girls can and do live very rich and fulfilling lives, even as they negotiate to stay within their prescribed roles. This is particularly evident in the area of entrepreneurship. Karen Johnson-Weiner has noted that "even as Amish women entrepreneurs reinforce community ties, some are building businesses that reach beyond the boundaries of their church communities, challenging traditional understanding of what it means to be a helpmeet, homemaker, and nurturer."[418]

The Amish are a constant reminder of a plain and simple lifestyle. *Cleveland Public Library/ Photograph Collection.*

Neither Dora nor Esther ever returned to the half-finished "basement house" where they lived at the time of Paul's murder, and it stood vacant for more than two years. Eventually, Dora's second cousin, John C. Miller, and his wife, Rebecca, moved into the dwelling, and a second story was added. Today, Pete Miller Sr. and his wife, Katie Miller, Paul's sister, occupy it. Esther went on to marry a Mount Eaton farmer in the mid-1970s. They would have nine children—not an especially large number for an Old Order Amish family.

We can only hope that both Dora and Esther were able to find the happiness that was once ripped away from them one terrible night in July 1957—and that the death of Paul Coblentz, like countless other martyrs before him, was not in vain.

NOTES

Introduction

1. A Baptist minister, John Leland was an important figure in the early struggle for religious liberty in the United States.
2. Kraybill et al., *Amish Grace*.
3. Hochstetler e-mail, December 21, 2019, in which he quotes his grandfather.
4. Goeringer, *Haunts of Violence in the Church*.
5. Ibid.
6. Amish America, "Amish America Q-and-A."
7. Olsen, *Killing in Amish Country*.
8. II Corinthians 6:14.
9. Johnson-Weiner, "Keepers at Home?"
10. Ibid., "Role of Women."
11. *Cumulative Book Review Digest*.
12. It is a play on the term "bodice ripper," which is shorthand for a particular genre of romance novels.
13. Martin, "'Rosanna' Reconsidered."

Chapter 1

14. Some sources say it was 180 acres.
15. Miller, *Tragedies Along County Road 235*.

16. Although his headstone is inscribed Moses J. Coblentz, in life he was always known as "Mose."
17. Enticed by cheap land, some Ohio Amish began moving to Iowa as early as 1840.
18. Bowman, *Mt. Hope.*
19. Stebbins, "Continue Hunt for 2 Killers."
20. Ibid.
21. "Ana" is Greek for "again"—to baptize again.
22. Owing to the high birth rate and declining infant mortality, the Amish are one of the fastest-growing faith-based groups in the United States.
23. Bronner, *Youth Culture in America.*
24. *Signifying: The Education of Levi Miller,* "1957 Baptism and Murder."
25. Ibid.
26. Ibid.
27. Miller, *Tragedies Along County Road 235.*
28. Ward, "Thugs Shatter Calm Amish Community."
29. Ibid.
30. Noos, *Coping with Life Crises.*
31. Miller, "Amish Funeral."
32. Ward, "Thugs Shatter Calm Amish Community."
33. *Mennonite Weekly Review,* "Apprehend Two Young Men for Slaying."
34. *Columbus (OH) Dispatch,* "Rites Held for Slain Amish Man."
35. *Holmes County (OH) Farmer-Hub,* undated.
36. *Columbus (OH) Dispatch,* "Rites Held for Slain Amish Man."
37. Miller, "Amish Funeral."
38. Ibid.
39. Hochstetler e-mail, December 21, 2019.

Chapter 2

40. An early Christian author, Tertullian is sometimes called "the founder of Western theology."
41. *Delphos (OH) Daily Herald,* "Peculiar Ohio Community."
42. II Corinthians 6:17.
43. Hostetler, *Descendants of Jacob Hochstetler.*
44. Newton, *History of Holmes County, Ohio.*
45. Hostetler, *Descendants of Jacob Hochstetler.*
46. Ibid.

47. Ibid.
48. *Stark County (OH) Democrat*, "Murderer Confined in the Knox County Jail."
49. *Holmes County (OH) Farmer*, February 17, 1876.
50. Meyers and Meyers Walker, *Lynching and Mob Violence in Ohio*.
51. *Evening Independent* (Massillon, OH), "Murder Trial New for Holmes County."
52. Henry told a reporter he was Lutheran.
53. *Columbus (OH) Dispatch*, "Amish People."
54. Ibid.
55. Ibid.
56. *Fort Scott (KS) Weekly Monitor*, "Suffer in Silence."
57. Ibid.
58. Meyers and Meyers Walker, *Lynching and Mob Violence in Ohio*.
59. *Columbus (OH) Dispatch*, "Amish People."
60. Ibid.
61. *Democratic Northwest and Henry County (OH) News*, "Another Fake."
62. Meyers and Meyers Walker, *Lynching and Mob Violence in Ohio*.
63. *Marysville (OH) Journal-Tribune*, "Tarred and Feathered."
64. *Democratic Banner* (Mt. Vernon, OH), "Mob."
65. In 2011, a breakaway Amish cult led by Samuel Mullet Sr. conducted a series of attacks on Amish men in Holmes County, forcibly cutting off their hair and beards. Mullet and fifteen others were sentenced to prison for this rare instance of Amish-on-Amish violence.
66. *Daily Times* (New Philadelphia, OH), "Phantom Bandit Robs 3 More."
67. *Daily Reporter* (Dover, OH), "Amish Youth Is Victim of Gang Attack."
68. Ibid.
69. "Claping" is thought to be derived from the derogatory term "clay apes," which is sometimes used to describe the Amish.

Chapter 3

70. Doerfler, "Musical Life in Holmes County, Ohio."
71. Alderman, *Secret Life of the Lawman's Wife*.
72. Doerfler, "Musical Life in Holmes County, Ohio."
73. Ibid.
74. Alderman, *Secret Life of the Lawman's Wife*.
75. Doerfler, "Musical Life in Holmes County, Ohio."

76. Alderman, *Secret Life of the Lawman's Wife*.
77. *Leader-Telegram* (Eau Claire, WI), "Prisoners 'Accompany' Sheriff Who Led Band."
78. *Coshocton (OH) Tribune*, "Just Who's Crazy?"
79. *News-Journal* (Mansfield, OH), "Holmes Sheriff Arrested!"
80. *Coshocton (OH) Tribune*, "Just Who's Crazy?"
81. Miller, *Tragedies Along County Road 235*.
82. Ibid.
83. Ibid.
84. *Coshocton (OH) News*, "Fredericksburg Amish Boy Found Dead."
85. *Daily Times* (New Philadelphia, OH), "Grand Jurors Indict Weiss."
86. And again from 1965 until 1967, when his son, Darryl, took over.
87. Doerfler, "Musical Life in Holmes County, Ohio."
88. Gingerich, the father of ten, claimed that his wife refused to cook for him or permit him to eat at the same table. He appears to have been mentally unstable and was committed to the Massillon State Hospital for several years. At the time of his death, he had left the Amish and become a Mennonite.
89. Petrovich, "More than Forty Amish Affiliations?"
90. Stoltzfus, *Amish Confidential*.
91. Olsen, *Killing in Amish Country*.
92. Petrovich lived among the Old Order Amish in Allen County, Indiana, and eventually joined the emerging New Order Amish church.
93. The others are Lancaster County, Pennsylvania; Elkhart–LaGrange County, Indiana; Geauga County, Ohio; and Adams County, Indiana.
94. Wikipedia, "Dordrecht Confession of Faith."
95. Johnson-Weiner, "On the Amish and Shunning."
96. Petrovich, "More than Forty Amish Affiliations?"
97. Except when he had to arrest John W. Helmuth for shooting a neighbor's bull.

Chapter 4

98. The last of the "Five Good [Roman] Emperors," Aurelius was also a highly regarded philosopher.
99. Bowman, *Mt. Hope*.
100. Ibid.
101. Miller, *Tragedies Along County Road 235*.

102. The car was variously described as cream and gray, cream and blue and blue-green.

103. *Ohio State Journal* (Columbus), "Extend Search in Amish Killing."

104. Ibid.

105. Miller, *Tragedies Along County Road 235*.

106. *Columbus (OH) Citizen*, "Killers Left Prints on Wife's Glasses."

107. *Ohio State Journal* (Columbus), "Charge 2 in Slaying of Amish Farmer."

108. Miller, *Tragedies Along County Road 235*.

109. Ibid.

110. *Evening Independent* (Massillon, OH), "Search Illinois Swamp for Murder Suspect."

111. Ibid.

112. *News-Journal* (Mansfield, OH), "Nab 2 Suspects in Amish Killing."

113. *Evening Independent* (Massillon, OH), "Search Illinois Swamp for Murder Suspect."

114. Ibid.

115. Miller, *Tragedies Along County Road 235*.

116. Gerald F. "Jerry" Knapp would later be appointed a deputy sheriff by Weiss, while continuing to operate his tavern.

117. Miller, *Tragedies Along County Road 235*.

118. Ibid.

119. *Columbus (OH) Citizen*, "Slaying Suspects Held in Illinois."

120. Dumoulin telephone interview, February 7, 2020.

121. A former Millersburg fire chief and musician, Theodore "Ted" Geib would soon become a full-time deputy under Weiss.

122. *Daily Reporter* (Dover, OH), "Amish Boy's Wounds."

123. *Daily Reporter* (Dover, OH), "Return 2 Slayers to Holmes County."

124. *Daily Times* (New Philadelphia, OH), "Amish Murder Victim's Widow to Face Killers."

125. Ibid.

126. Norris, *Federal Correctional Institution*.

127. Greene, "Prisons without Walls Helping Many Youths."

128. *Daily Times* (New Philadelphia, OH), "Amish Murder Victim's Widow."

129. *Columbus (OH) Citizen*, "Youth, 19, Found Guilty of Murder."

130. Butler, "Peters Doesn't Know Why He Got into 'Mess.'"

131. Ibid.

132. It was the Holmesville Lumber Company until 1952.

133. *Columbus (OH) Dispatch*, "Pair Hoped to Murder Sheriff."

134. Ibid.

135. Ibid.

136. *Marysville (OH) Journal-Tribune*, "Amishman's Killers Separated in Jail."

137. *Columbus (OH) Dispatch*, "Pair Hoped to Murder Sheriff."

138. *News-Journal* (Mansfield, OH), "Pair Ruled Sane; Face Trial in Amish Slaying."

Chapter 5

139. White, "Terror at the Amish Farmhouse."

140. Undated newspaper clipping, Holmes County Historical Society.

141. *Columbus (OH) Dispatch*, "Amish Murder Trial to Begin."

142. *Lancaster (OH) Eagle-Gazette*, "Korean Vet's Life Spared by Governor."

143. *Columbus (OH) Dispatch*, "Brown Raps Lausche in Issuing Pardons."

144. *Columbus (OH) Dispatch*, "Amish Murder Trial to Begin."

145. Ibid.

146. *Recorder* (Zanesville, OH), "Parker Trial in Holmes County."

147. Ibid.

148. When author David Meyers worked in the psychology department at the Ohio State Reformatory, Lima routinely declared that there was nothing wrong with the inmates we sent there for evaluation, even when they were clearly schizophrenic. It became a joke.

149. *Coshocton (OH) Tribune*, "Ohio Pen Alienists Declare Parker Insane."

150. *News-Journal* (Mansfield, OH), "Rapist Gets 3 Years at OSR on Birthday."

151. *News-Journal* (Mansfield, OH), "Holmes Amish Residents Attend Attack Arraignment."

152. Ibid.

153. Stebbins, "Defense Says Amish Slaying Suspect 'Drink-Crazed Boy.'"

154. Ibid.

155. Ibid., "Parents of Accused Closely Watch Murder Trial of Son."

156. Ibid.

157. *Daily Reporter* (Dover, OH), "Lawyer Asks Death Penalty in Millersburg."

158. Stebbins, "Amish Murder Trial to Begin."

159. Ibid., "Defense Says Amish Slaying Suspect 'Drink-Crazed Boy.'"

160. *Columbus (OH) Dispatch*, "Aviation Reporter."

161. *Daily Reporter* (Dover, OH), "10 Approved As Jurors in Slaying Trial."

162. Stebbins, "Defense Says Amish Slaying Suspect 'Drink-Crazed Boy.'"

163. Ibid., "Parents of Accused Closely Watch Murder Trial of Son."

164. Ibid., "Defense Says Amish Slaying Suspect 'Drink-Crazed Boy.'"

165. *Daily Reporter* (Dover, OH), "4 Testify in Murder Trial."

166. *State of Ohio v. Cleo Eugene Peters.*

167. *Daily Reporter* (Dover, OH), "4 Testify in Murder Trial."

Chapter 6

168. Landay is an award-winning crime/mystery novelist.

169. *State of Ohio v. Cleo Eugene Peters.*

170. Ibid.

171. Ibid.

172. Ibid.

173. Ibid.

174. *Daily Reporter* (Dover, OH), "4 Testify in Murder Trial."

175. *State of Ohio v. Cleo Eugene Peters.*

176. Presumably this was a battery-powered lamp.

177. *Daily Reporter* (Dover, OH), "4 Testify in Murder Trial."

178. *State of Ohio v. Cleo Eugene Peters.*

179. *Daily Reporter* (Dover, OH), "Slain Farmer's Father Describes Death Scene."

180. Ibid.

181. Stebbins, "Amish Man Tells of Son's Slaying."

182. "Thou shalt not make unto thee any graven image, or any likeness of any thing that is in heaven above, or that is in the earth beneath, or that is in the water under the earth," Exodus 20:4 (KJV).

183. *State of Ohio v. Cleo Eugene Peters.*

184. *Daily Reporter* (Dover, OH), "Slain Farmer's Father Describes Death Scene."

185. Ibid.

186. *State of Ohio v. Cleo Eugene Peters.*

187. Ibid.

188. Ibid.

189. Ibid.

190. *Carrol (IA) Daily Times Herald*, "Set Hearing on Iowan's 2 Slaying Confessions."

191. Stebbins, "Trial Airs Confession Argument."

192. Ibid.

193. *State of Ohio v. Cleo Eugene Peters.*

194. Ibid.
195. Ibid.
196. Ibid.
197. *Sandusky (OH) Register*, "Re-sentence of Peters Required."
198. Stebbins, "Peters Confession Upheld by Jurist."
199. *State of Ohio v. Cleo Eugene Peters.*
200. Ibid.
201. That was the alcohol content. It was sold to those who were under the age of twenty-one.
202. *State of Ohio v. Cleo Eugene Peters.*

Chapter 7

203. Omar Khayyam was a Persian mathematician, astronomer and poet.
204. *State of Ohio v. Cleo Eugene Peters.*
205. Ibid.
206. Ibid.
207. Ibid.
208. Stebbins, "Murder Case Ready for Jury."
209. *Sandusky (OH) Register*, "Re-sentence of Peters Required."
210. *State of Ohio v. Cleo Eugene Peters.*
211. Ibid.
212. *Sandusky (OH) Register*, "Re-sentence of Peters Required."
213. *State of Ohio v. Cleo Eugene Peters.*
214. Ibid.
215. Stebbins, "Murder Case Ready for Jury."
216. *State of Ohio v. Cleo Eugene Peters.*
217. Ibid.
218. Stebbins, "Murder Case Ready for Jury."
219. *State of Ohio v. Cleo Eugene Peters.*
220. Ibid.
221. Ibid.
222. Ibid.
223. Ibid.
224. Ibid.
225. Ibid.
226. Mrs. Murl Bell, Mrs. Hildred Smith, Mrs. Fred Mast, Mrs. Laura Augsburger, Mrs. Lula Frink, Mrs. Martha Haas, Harvey Sumney, James

Norman, Robert Schlegel, Bryce Lifer, Warren Massie, Arthur E. Parrot and H.E. Parsons (extra juror).

227. *Sandusky (OH) Register*, "Re-sentence of Peters Required."

228. Stebbins, "Peters Convicted, Must Die in Chair."

229. Ibid.

230. Ibid.

231. Ibid.

232. Ibid.

233. *Daily Times* (New Philadelphia, OH), "Resentence Peters to Die April 10."

234. *Columbus (OH) Citizen*, "Youth, 19, Found Guilty of Murder."

235. *Columbus (OH) Dispatch*, "Millersburg Trial."

Chapter 8

236. Eade is an America attorney and activist who also writes political and legal thrillers.

237. *Daily Reporter* (Dover, OH), "Wooster Attorney Quits Murder Case."

238. *Evening Independent* (Massillon, OH), "Holdup Men Rob Young Amishman."

239. *Columbus (OH) Dispatch*, "Millersburg Trial Will Open Monday."

240. Schmidt, "Who Is to Blame for JD?"

241. Ibid.

242. *Columbus (OH) Dispatch*, "Millersburg Trial Will Open Monday."

243. In the summer of 1953, Saint Aloysius closed.

244. Dumoulin telephone interview, January 8, 2020.

245. Ibid.

246. *Columbus (OH) Dispatch*, "Millersburg Trial Will Open Monday."

247. Dumoulin telephone interview, January 8, 2020.

248. *News-Journal* (Mansfield, OH), "Judges Go to Scene of Murder."

249. Ibid.

250. Ibid.

251. *News-Journal* (Mansfield, OH), "Widow Tells of Slaying."

252. Ibid.

253. Ibid.

254. Stebbins, "Dumoulin Pointed Out by Widow."

255. Ibid.

256. *News-Journal* (Mansfield, OH), "Widow Tells of Slaying."

257. *Daily Reporter* (Dover, OH), "Illinois Officers Awaited at Trial."
258. *State of Ohio v. Cleo Eugene Peters.*
259. Ibid.
260. Ibid.
261. Ibid.
262. Ibid.
263. *News-Journal* (Mansfield, OH), "Widow Tells of Slaying."
264. Ibid.
265. Ibid.
266. Undated file clipping, *Holmes County (OH) Farmer-Hub.*
267. *Daily Reporter* (Dover, OH), "Illinois Officers Awaited at Trial."
268. *Daily Chronicle* (DeKalb, IL), "Is Sentenced Yesterday on Murder Charge."
269. *News-Journal* (Mansfield, OH), "Await Two Witnesses."
270. *Times Recorder* (Zanesville, OH), "Youth Given Life Sentence."
271. *Daily Times* (New Philadelphia, OH), "To Place Youth in Solitary on Date of Murder."
272. Dumoulin telephone interview, January 8, 2020.
273. Ibid.
274. Ibid.
275. Ibid.
276. *Columbus (OH) Dispatch*, "Parents Hear Story."
277. Ibid.
278. Ibid.
279. Ibid.
280. Ibid.
281. Ibid.
282. *Times Recorder* (Zanesville, OH), "Judge Bars 'Confession' from Trial."
283. *Daily Reporter* (Dover, OH), "Illinois Officers Awaited at Trial."
284. Ibid.
285. Ibid.

Chapter 9

286. Synott, Dietzel and Loannou, "Review of the Polygraph."
287. *Times Recorder* (Zanesville, OH), "Youth Given Life Sentence."
288. *Daily Reporter* (Dover, OH), "Holmes Trial Ending Today."
289. Ibid.

290. Ibid.

291. We have corrected punctuation, spelling and formatting because there appeared to be some clerical errors, but we did not have access to the original document to confirm.

292. *Holmes County (OH) Farmer-Hub*, undated clipping from Holmes County Historical Society.

293. Mike continues to claim that he did not harm either one, although Dora's dress was clearly torn and she bore some marks on her face.

294. Stebbins, "Dumoulin Given Life Term in Pen."

295. Ibid.

296. Ibid.

297. *Times Recorder* (Zanesville, OH), "Youth Given Life Sentence."

298. *Daily Times* (New Philadelphia, OH), "Dumoulin Given Life in Slaying."

299. Ibid.

300. Ibid.

301. *Daily Reporter* (Dover, OH), "Coblentz Salyer's Pal Receives Life Sentence."

Chapter 10

302. Bruce was an American stand-up comedian who pioneered in social satire during the 1950s and early '60s.

303. Bisbort, "Curious Case of Caryl Chessman."

304. *To Abolish the Death Penalty*.

305. *Columbus (OH) Dispatch*, "O'Neill Gets His First Condemned Slayer Case."

306. *Columbus (OH) Dispatch*, "Patrolman's Killer Is Executed."

307. Ibid.

308. It is now known simply as Alvis.

309. *Daily Reporter* (Dover, OH), "Second Amish Murder Trial Starts Feb. 3."

310. *Columbus (OH) Dispatch*, "Logan Wife Slayer Reads Bible."

311. Johnson gave up his pastorship one year later.

312. Butler, "Peters Doesn't Know Why He Got into 'Mess.'"

313. *Columbus (OH) Dispatch*, "Tannyhill to Be 300th Chair Victim."

314. *Columbus (OH) Dispatch*, "Vaughns Dies in Pen Chair."

315. Lore, "Inside the Pen."

316. *Columbus (OH) Dispatch*, "Execution Stay Granted Peters."

317. Butler, "Peters Doesn't Know Why He Got into 'Mess.'"

318. Ibid.
319. Ibid.
320. Ibid.
321. Ibid.
322. *Marysville (OH) Journal-Tribune*, "Final Plans Made for Pair Convicted of Murder."
323. Ibid.
324. Beiler, *Think No Evil.*
325. Russell, *Overcoming Evil God's Way.*
326. Ibid.
327. *Signifying: The Education of Levi Miller*, "1957 Baptism and Murder."
328. Kraybill et al., *Amish Grace.*
329. *Signifying: The Education of Levi Miller*, "1957 Baptism and Murder."
330. *News-Journal* (Mansfield, OH), "Governor Spares Life of Youthful Slayer."
331. Ibid.
332. Ibid.
333. Ibid.
334. Ibid.
335. Ibid.
336. *Columbus (OH) Dispatch*, "Car Crash Slayer Dies in Chair."
337. *Columbus (OH) Dispatch*, "DiSalle Cites Reaction to Execution."

Chapter 11

338. *Daily Reporter* (Dover, OH), "Corrections Unit Unveils Improvements Program."
339. Stebbins, "Dumoulin Give Life Term in Pen."
340. "Stir" is inmate slang for being imprisoned.
341. Dumoulin telephone interview, February 7, 2020.
342. *Times Recorder* (Zanesville, OH), "Ohio Pen's Oldest Prisoner."
343. Craig, "Convict, 94, Leaves Pen."
344. *Columbus (OH) Dispatch*, "Warden and Solly Hart Injured."
345. Cowie, "Ohio Pen Break by 4 Foiled."
346. Ibid.
347. *Evening Review* (East Liverpool, OH), "Alvis Probes 'Small Riot' at Ohio Pen."
348. Dumoulin telephone interview, January 8, 2020.

349. *Columbus (OH) Dispatch*, "Death Ends Terms of 77 Lifers."

350. Blakeslee, "Hopeful Gains Made in Battle Against Cancer."

351. *Columbus (OH) Dispatch*, "Test Tranquilizers on Ohio Pen Volunteers."

352. *Columbus (OH) Dispatch*, "15 at Pen Volunteer for Tests."

353. *Columbus (OH) Dispatch*, "Probe Ordered into Claim Licavoli Gets Privileges."

354. *Columbus (OH) Dispatch*, "Licavoli Returned to Pen in Expose."

355. Warden Thomas had demonstrated his incompetence during the 1930 prison fire. See Meyers, Meyers Walker and Dailey, *Inside the Ohio Penitentiary*.

356. *Columbus (OH) Dispatch*, "Probe Ordered into Claim Licavoli Gets Privileges."

357. Ibid.

358. *Columbus (OH) Dispatch*, "Alvis Will Release Licavoli Data Friday."

359. Dumoulin telephone interview, January 8, 2020.

360. Ibid.

361. Ibid.

362. Encyclopedia.com, "King, Don 1931–."

363. *Lancaster (OH) Eagle-Gazette*, "Ohio's Prison Population Has Shrunk Since '65."

Chapter 12

364. Spoken by Ophelia in Shakespeare's *Hamlet*.

365. Beiler, *Think No Evil*.

366. *Gospel Herald* 52.

367. Russell, *Overcoming Evil God's Way*.

368. *Iowa City (IA) Press-Citizen*, "Mennonites Will Study Criticism of Death Penalty."

369. Ibid.

370. DiSalle, "Comments on Capital Punishment and Clemency."

371. Ibid.

372. *Sentencing in Capital Cases*.

373. *Capital Punishment: Hearings*.

374. Miller, *Tragedies Along County Road 235*.

375. Dumoulin telephone interview, January 8, 2020.

376. Dumoulin telephone interview, February 7, 2020.

377. Ibid.

378. Ibid.
379. Ibid.
380. Ibid.
381. Ibid.
382. Ibid.
383. Ibid.
384. Ibid.
385. *Daily Reporter* (Dover, OH), "Prosecutor Says Felons Should at Least Serve Minimum Sentences."
386. Dumoulin telephone interview, February 7, 2020.
387. Dumoulin telephone interview, January 8, 2020.
388. Dumoulin telephone interview, February 7, 2020.
389. *Daily Review Atlas* (Monmouth, IL), "Cleo Eugene 'Gene' Peters."
390. Dumoulin telephone interview, February 7, 2020.
391. Harry Weiss passed away on August 17, 1989, at the age of ninety-one.
392. Dumoulin telephone interview, January 8, 2020.
393. Amy Gerber Doerfler e-mail, March 23, 2020.

Chapter 13

394. The Amish regard themselves as "the quiet in the land."
395. Johnson-Weiner, "Keepers at Home?"
396. Zellner, *Sects, Cults, and Spiritual Communities.*
397. Ibid.
398. Hochstetler e-mail, December 21, 2019.
399. King, *Joys, Sorrows, and Shadows.*
400. Miller, *Tragedies Along County Road 235.*
401. Ibid.
402. Ibid.
403. Ibid.
404. Ibid.
405. *Daily Reporter* (Dover, OH), "2 Injured in Fall in Farm Mishap."
406. *Daily Reporter* (Dover, OH), "Henry Yoder."
407. Hurst, *Amish Paradox.*
408. Zellner, *Sects, Cults, and Spiritual Communities.*
409. King, *Joys, Sorrows, and Shadows.*
410. Ibid.
411. Seifter et al., "Analysis of the Bereavement Effect.

412. Hurst, *Amish Paradox*.

413. Ibid.

414. Zellner, *Sects, Cults, and Spiritual Communities*.

415. As of 2010, 5.3 percent of Amish women in Holmes County had lost their spouses, compared to only 0.4 percent of the men. This imbalance is skewed even further by the need to marry within one's particular church.

416. Hurst, *Amish Paradox*.

417. Wagler, *Growing Up Amish*.

418. Johnson-Weiner, "Keepers at Home?"

BIBLIOGRAPHY

Books

Alderman, BJ. *The Secret Life of the Lawman's Wife*. Westport, CT: Praeger, 2007.

Beiler, Jonas, with Shawn Smucker. *Think No Evil: Inside the Story of the Amish Schoolhouse Shooting…and Beyond*. New York: Howard Books. 2009.

Bowman, Eli H. *Mt. Hope, A Pictorial History, 1824–1999*. Walnut Creek, OH: Carlisle Publishing, 1999.

Bronner, Simon J., and Cindy Dell Clark, eds. *Youth Culture in America*. Santa Barbara, CA: Greenwood, 2016.

Capital Punishment: Hearings Before the Subcommittee on Criminal Justice. No. 133. Washington, D.C.: U.S. Government Printing Office, 1987.

The Cumulative Book Review Digest. Minneapolis, MN: H.W. Wilson Company, 1905.

Goeringer, Howard. *Haunts of Violence in the Church*. West Conshohocken, PA: Infinity Publishing Company, 2005.

Hostetler, Harvey. *Descendants of Jacob Hochstetler, the Immigrant of 1736*. Elgin, IL: Brethren Publishing House, 1912.

Hurst, Charles E., and David L. McConnell. *An Amish Paradox*. Baltimore, MD: Johns Hopkins University Press, 2010.

King, Emma. *Joys, Sorrows, and Shadows*. Elverson, PA: Olde Springfield Shoppe, 1992.

Kraybill, Donald B., Steven M. Nolt and David L. Weaver-Zercher. *Amish Grace: How Forgiveness Transcended Tragedy*. San Francisco, CA: Josey-Bass, 2007.

————. *The Amish Way: Patient Faith in a Perilous World*. San Francisco, CA: Jossey-Bass, 2010.

Meyers, David, and Elise Meyers. *Central Ohio's Historic Prisons*. Charleston, SC: Arcadia Publishing, 2009.

Meyers, David, and Elise Meyers Walker. *Lynching and Mob Violence in Ohio, 1772–1938*. Jefferson, NC: McFarland & Company Inc., 2019.

Meyers, David, Elise Meyers Walker and James Dailey II. *Inside the Ohio Penitentiary*. Charleston, SC: The History Press, 2013.

Miller, John C. *Tragedies Along County Road 235*. Walnut Creek, OH: Carlisle Publishing, 2008.

Noos, R.H., ed. *Coping with Life Crises*. Boston: Springer, 1979.

Norris, J.T., Jr. *The Federal Correctional Institution, Ashland, Kentucky*. Ashland, KY: Ashland Daily Independent, 1951.

Olsen, Gregg, and Rebecca Morris. *A Killing in Amish Country*. New York: St. Martin's Press, 2016.

Perrin, William Henry. *History of Morrow County and Ohio*. Chicago: O.L. Baskin & Company, 1880.

Russell, Stephen. *Overcoming Evil God's Way: The Biblical and Historical Case for Nonresistance*. Guys Mills, PA: Faith Builders Resource Group, 2008.

Sartre, Jean Paul. *No Exit*. New York: Samuel French Inc., 1958.

Sentencing in Capital Cases: Hearings Before the Subcommittee on Criminal Justice. Washington, D.C.: U.S. Government Printing Office, 1978.

Smucker, Esther F. *Good Night, My Son: A Treasure in Heaven*. Morgantown, PA: Masthof Press, 1995.

State of Ohio v. Cleo Eugene Peters. Millersburg, OH: Holmes County Common Pleas Court, 1957. Trial transcript.

Stoltzfus, "Lebanon" Levi. *Amish Confidential*. New York: Gallery Books, 2015.

To Abolish the Death Penalty: Hearings Before the Subcommittee on Criminal Laws and Procedures. Washington, D.C.: U.S. Government Printing Office, 1970.

Wagler, Ira. *Growing Up Amish*. Carol Steam, IL: Tyndale House Publishers Inc., 2011.

Zellner, William W., and Marc Petrowsky. *Sects, Cults, and Spiritual Communities*. Westport, CT: Praeger, 1998.

Articles and Other Sources

Amish America. "An Amish America Q-and-A with Professor Karen Johnson-Weiner: Part Two." https://amishamerica.com/an-amish-america-q-and-a-with-professor-karen-johnson-weiner-part-two.

Bisbort, Alan. "The Curious Case of Caryl Chessman." Gadfly Online, October 29, 2001. http://www.gadflyonline.com/home/10-29-01/ftr-caryl-chessman.html.

Blakeslee, Alton L. "Hopeful Gains Made in Battle Against Cancer." *Columbus (OH) Dispatch*, January 19, 1958.

Butler, Bernard H. "Peters Doesn't Know Why He Got into 'Mess.'" *Sandusky (OH) Register*, May 21, 1958.

Carrol (IA) Daily Times Herald. "Set Hearing on Iowan's 2 Slaying Confessions." December 9, 1957.

Columbus (OH) Citizen. "Killers Left Prints on Wife's Glasses." July 20, 1957.

———. "Slaying Suspects Held in Illinois." July 23, 1957.

———. "Youth, 19, Found Guilty of Murder." December 12, 1957.

Columbus (OH) Dispatch. "Alvis Will Release Licavoli Data Friday." December 25, 1958.

———. "Amish Murder Trial to Begin." December 1, 1957.

———. "The Amish People." June 4, 1895.

———. "Aviation Reporter Had a Bird's-Eye View of the History of Flight." April 30, 2005.

———. "Brown Raps Lausche in Issuing Pardons." January 12, 1957.

———. "Car Crash Slayer Dies in Chair." December 20, 1958.

———. "Death Ends Terms of 77 Lifers at Ohio Pen, Farm." March 21, 1958.

———. "DiSalle Cites Reaction to Execution." July 8, 1959.

———. "Execution Stay Granted Peters." March 6, 1958.

———. "15 at Pen Volunteer for Tests." May 13, 1957.

———. "Licavoli Returned to Pen in Expose." November 7, 1958.

———. "Logan Wife Slayer Reads Bible in Cell on Death Row." January 20, 1955.

———. "The Millersburg Trial." December 13, 1957.

———. "Millersburg Trial Will Open Monday." February 2, 1957.

———. "O'Neill Gets His First Condemned Slayer Case." June 7, 1957.

———. "Pair Hoped to Murder Sheriff." July 26, 1957.

———. "Parents Hear Story of Son's Part in Amish Murder." February 5, 1958.

———. "Patrolman's Killer Is Executed." January 4, 1958.

———. "Probe Ordered into Claim Licavoli Gets Privileges." November 6, 1958

———. "Rites Held for Slain Amish Man." July 23, 1957.

———. "Tannyhill to Be 300th Chair Victim." October 16, 1955.

———. "Test Tranquilizers on Ohio Pen Volunteers." October 27, 1958.

———. "Vaughns Dies in Pen Chair." March 1, 1958.

———. "Warden and Solly Hart Injured in Auto Crash." January 29, 1958.

Columbus (OH) Star. "Thugs Shatter Calm Amish Community." July 27, 1957.

Coshocton (OH) News. "Fredericksburg Amish Boy Found Dead in Automobile." March 11, 1946.

Coshocton (OH) Tribune. "Aliens Here Must Turn in Radios, Guns, Cameras." January 4, 1942.

———. "Just Who's Crazy?" February 17, 1937.

———. "Ohio Pen Alienists Declare Parker Insane." April 12, 1933.

Cowie, Jack. "Ohio Pen Break by 4 Foiled." *Columbus (OH) Dispatch*, February 22, 1958.

Craig, Jimmy. "Convict, 94, Leaves Pen After Serving 30 Years for Murder." *Columbus (OH) Dispatch*, January 23, 1958.

Daily Chronicle (DeKalb, IL). "Is Sentenced Yesterday on Murder Charge." February 7, 1958.

Daily Record (Wooster, OH). "Along Ohio 39: Ax-Handle Murder Put Berlin in Limelight." September 9, 1966.

Daily Reporter (Dover, OH). "Amish Boy's Wounds Touch Off Brief Flurry in Millersburg." July 24, 1957.

———. "Amish Youth Is Victim of Gang Attack." May 11, 1957.

———. "Coblentz Slayer's Pal Receives Life Sentence." February 7, 1958.

———. "Corrections Unit Unveils Improvements Program." September 25, 1958.

———. "4 Testify in Murder Trial." December 5, 1957.

———. "Henry Yoder." January 21, 1972.

———. "Holmes Trial Ending Today." February 6, 1958.

———. "Illinois Officers Awaited at Trial." February 5, 1958.

———. "Lawyer Asks Death Penalty in Millersburg." December 2, 1957.

———. "Prosecutor Says Felons Should at Least Serve Minimum Sentences Before Parole." September 6, 1973.

———. "Return 2 Slayers to Holmes County." July 23, 1957.

———. "Second Amish Murder Trial Starts Feb. 3." January 9, 1958.

———. "Slain Farmer's Father Describes Death Scene." December 6, 1957.

———. "10 Approved as Jurors in Slaying Trial." December 3, 1957.

———. "2 Injured in Fall in Farm Mishap." June 10, 1963.

———. "Wooster Attorney Quits Murder Case." June 24, 1955.

Daily Review Atlas (Monmouth, IL). "Cleo Eugene 'Gene' Peters, 1938–2015." August 6, 2015.

Daily Times (New Philadelphia, OH). "Amish Murder Victim's Widow to Face Killers; Officers Ban Cameramen." July 25, 1957.

———. "Dumoulin Given Life in Slaying." February 7. 1958.

———. "Grand Jurors Indict Weiss." September 19, 1946.

———. "Phantom Bandit Robs 3 More in Amish Buggies; Sect Curbs Night Travel." November 13, 1953

———. "Resentence Peters to Die April 10." December 12, 1957.

———. "To Place Youth in Solitary on Date of Murder." February 7, 1958.

———. "Two Arrested in Eagles' Club Raid." March 27, 1946.

Delphos (OH) Daily Herald. "A Peculiar Ohio Community." July 21, 1897.

Democratic Banner (Mount Vernon, OH). "Mob." June 23, 1911.

Democratic Northwest and Henry County (OH) News. "Another Fake." July 4, 1895.

DiSalle, Michael V. "Comments on Capital Punishment and Clemency." *Ohio State Law Journal* 25 (1964).

Doerfler, Amy Gerber. "Musical Life in Holmes County, Ohio, from 1917–1960." Our Town, Holmes County, Ohio. https://ourtownholmes. wordpress.com/tag/weiss.

Dumoulin, Mike. Telephone interview with David Meyers, February 7, 2020.

———. Telephone interview with David Meyers, January 8, 2020.

Edwardsville (IL) Intelligencer. "Murder Suspect Returned to Ohio." July 24, 1957.

Encyclopedia.com. "King, Don 1931–." https://www.encyclopedia.com/ people/sports-and-games/sports-biographies/don-king#E.

Evening Independent (Massillon, OH). "Holdup Men Rob Young Amishman." February 1, 1958.

———. "Murder Trial New for Holmes County." March 24, 1930.

———. "Search Illinois Swamp for Murder Suspect." July 22, 1957.

Evening Review (East Liverpool, OH). "Alvis Probes 'Small Riot' at Ohio Pen." March 25, 1958.

Ferketich, Amy K., et al. "Tobacco Use Among the Amish in Holmes County, Ohio." *Journal of Rural Health* (February 1, 2008). https://onlinelibrary. wiley.com/doi/full/10.1111/j.1748-0361.2008.00141.x.

Fort Scott (KS) Weekly Monitor. "Suffer in Silence." July 27, 1895.

Gospel Herald 52, no. 27 (July 14, 1959).

Greene, Roger. "Prisons without Walls Helping Many Youths." *Corpus Christi (TX) Caller-Times*, December 30, 1956.

Hochstetler, Abraham "Amish Abe." E-mail, December 21, 2019.

Holmes County (OH) Farmer. February 17, 1876.

The Holmes County (OH) Farmer-Hub. Undated files at Holmes County Historical Society.

Hummel Group. "Our History." https://www.hummelgrp.com/about-us/our-history.

Iowa City (IA) Press-Citizen. "Mennonites Will Study Criticism of Death Penalty." August 23, 1963.

Johnson-Weiner, Karen M. "Keepers at Home? Amish Women and Entrepreneurship." *American Studies Journal*, no. 63 (2017). http://www.asjournal.org/63-2017/keepers-at-home-amish-women-and-entrepreneurship.

———. "On the Amish and Shunning." *John Hopkins University Press Blog*, February 3, 2014. https://www.jhupressblog.com/2014/02/03/on-the-amish-and-shunning-2.

———. "The Role of Women in Old Order Amish, Beachy Amish and Fellowship Churches." *Mennonite Quarterly Review* 75, no. 2 (April 2001).

Lancaster (OH) Eagle-Gazette. "Korean Vet's Life Spared by Governor." December 3, 1956.

———. "Ohio's Prison Population Has Shrunk Since '65." March 8, 1973.

Leader-Telegram (Eau Claire, WI). "Prisoners 'Accompany' Sheriff Who Led Band." February 21, 1935.

Lore, David. "Inside the Pen." *Columbus (OH) Dispatch*, October 28, 1984.

Marion (OH) Star. "Charges Filed Against Pair in Amish Farmer's Slaying." July 23, 1957.

Martin, Heidi. "'Rosanna' Reconsidered." *Mennonite World Review*, March 30, 2009.

Marysville (OH) Journal-Tribune. "Amishman's Killers Separated in Jail." July 26, 1957.

———. "Final Plans Made for Pair Convicted of Murder." October 29, 1958.

———. "Tarred and Feathered." June 22, 1911.

Mennonite Weekly Review. "Apprehend Two Young Men for Slaying in Holmes County, Ohio." August 1, 1957.

Miller, Rebecca. "An Amish Funeral: A Firsthand Account." *Amish America*, July 14, 2015. https://amishamerica.com/amish-funeral-firsthand-account.

News-Journal (Mansfield, OH). "Await Two Witnesses." February 5, 1958.

————. "Governor Spares Life of Youthful Slayer." November 7, 1958.

————. "Holmes Amish Residents Attend Attack Arraignment." January 13, 1949.

————. "Holmes Sheriff Arrested! It's All Joke on Deputy." February 17, 1937.

————. "Judges Go to Scene of Murder." February 3, 1958.

————. "Nab 2 Suspects in Amish Killing." July 22, 1957.

————. "Pair Ruled Sane; Face Trial in Amish Slaying." October 19, 1957.

————. "Rapist Gets 3 Years at OSR on Birthday." October 27, 1948.

————. "Widow Tells of Slaying." February 4, 1958.

Newton, George F. "History of Holmes County, Ohio." Millersburg, OH: Holmes County Library, 1889. Unpublished manuscript.

Ohio State Journal (Columbus). "Charge 2 in Slaying of Amish Farmer." July 23, 1957.

————. "Extend Search in Amish Killing." July 20, 1957.

Petrovich, Christopher. "More than Forty Amish Affiliations? Charting the Fault Lines." *Journal of Amish and Plain Anabaptist Studies* 2, no. 1 (2017).

Recorder (Zanesville, OH). "Parker Trial in Holmes County to Open Wednesday." January 9, 1933.

Sandusky (OH) Register. "Re-sentence of Peters Required." December 12, 1957.

Schmidt, J.P. "Who Is to Blame for JD?" *National 4-H Club News* 33, no. 6 (June 1955).

Seifter, Ari, Sarabdeep Singh, Patrick F. McArdle, Kathleen A. Ryan, Alan R. Shuldiner, Braxton D. Mitchell and Alejandro A. Schaffer. "Analysis of the Bereavement Effect After the Death of a Spouse." *BMJ Open,* July 26, 2013.

Signifying: The Education of Levi Miller. "1957 Baptism and Murder." http://levimillersignifying.blogspot.com/2014/11/1957-baptism-and-murder.html.

Stark County (OH) Democrat. "A Murderer Confined in the Knox County Jail." March 2, 1876.

Stebbins, Clair. "Amish Man Tells of Son's Slaying." *Columbus (OH) Dispatch,* December 6, 1957.

————. "Amish Murder Trial to Begin." *Columbus (OH) Dispatch,* December 1, 1957.

————. "Continue Hunt for 2 Killers." *Columbus (OH) Dispatch,* July 20, 1957.

———. "Defense Says Amish Slaying Suspect 'Drink-Crazed Boy.'" *Columbus (OH) Dispatch*, December 3, 1957.

———. "Defense Seeks to Delete Confession in Amish Slaying." *Columbus (OH) Dispatch*, December 5, 1957.

———. "Dumoulin Given Life Term in Pen." *Columbus (OH) Dispatch*, February 7, 1958.

———. "Dumoulin Pointed Out by Widow." *Columbus (OH) Dispatch*, February 4, 1958.

———. "Murder Case Ready for Jury." *Columbus (OH) Dispatch*, December 11, 1957.

———. "Parents of Accused Closely Watch Murder Trial of Son." *Columbus (OH) Dispatch*, December 3, 1957.

———. "Peters Confession Upheld by Jurist." *Columbus (OH) Dispatch*, December 10, 1957.

———. "Peters Convicted, Must Die in Chair." *Columbus (OH) Dispatch*, December 12, 1957.

———. "Trial Airs Confession Argument." *Columbus (OH) Dispatch*, December 8, 1957.

Synott, John, David Dietzel and Maria Loannou. "A Review of the Polygraph: History, Methodology and Current Status." *Crime Psychology Review* 1, no. 1 (2015).

Times Recorder (Zanesville, OH). "Judge Bars 'Confession' from Trial." February 5, 1958.

———. "Ohio Pen's Oldest Prisoner, 94, Is Granted Parole; To Get News Today at Junction City." December 11, 1957.

———. "Youth Given Life Sentence for Slaying Amish Farmer." February 7, 1958.

Ward, Frank H. "Thugs Shatter Calm Amish Community." *Columbus (OH) Star*, July 27, 1957.

White, Hal. "Terror at the Amish Farmhouse." *True Detective*, November 1957.

Wikipedia. "Dordrecht Confession of Faith." https://en.wikipedia.org/wiki/Dordrecht_Confession_of_Faith.

INDEX

INDEX

Hanna, W.S. 68
Harpster, Harvey 153
Harsh, R.C. 81
Hart, Solly 134
Hattery, Donald 127
Heilman, Michael 39, 40
Hershberger, Andrew 61
Hershberger, John 61
Hershberger, Levi 83
Hershberger, Monroe 61
Hershberger, Susan 156
High, Luther 23, 81, 82, 110, 116
Hileman, Michael 40
Hochstetler, Abraham 30, 155
Hochstetler, Anna 34
Hochstetler, David 34
Hochstetler, Jacob 34
Hochstetler, John 35
Hochstetler, Solomon 34, 35, 36
Hochstetler, Susan 35
Homan, Mrs. Don 54
Hostetler, John 49
Hostetler, Mahlon 72
Howerton, Thomas 111, 112
Hummel, Paul 126
Hunsberger, Mabel 145
Hunter, Manning 81, 107
Huyard, Naomi 156

J

Jackson, Robert 124
Johnson, Walter 121
Johnson-Weiner, Karen 14, 15, 49, 51, 154, 161
Jones, Charles 103
Jones, Ernest, Jr. 103

K

Kauffman, Atlee 22
Keeler, Leonarde 111
Keim, Mose 27, 28
Kendall, Wiley 81
King, Don 140

King, Emma 156, 159
Kline, Vernon 28
Knapp, Gerald 88
Knapp, Jerry 58
Knowles, Theodore 59
Koblenz, Maury 131, 135
Koloski, Marion 134
Kraybill, Donald 13, 49
Kuhn, Arden 44

L

Landis, Frank 103
Lausche, Frank 70, 118
Lawson, John Howard 62
Leech, Lloyd 103
Lehman, Barbara 35, 36
Lehman, Peter 25
Leyman, Dora 42
Licavoli, Thomas 136, 138
Lions, Tom 34
Livecchia, Gayle 160
Lore, David 123
Luedens, Henry 65

M

Maltz, Albert 62
Manley, Isha 101
Marino, Roy 134
Martin, Helen 15
Mast, Jacob 28, 36
Mast, Sarah 46
McClintock, C.B. 123
McClory, Bernard 127
McCrocklin, Leona 122
McKee, William 149
McKinley, William 39
McLaughlin, Dean 123
Meeker, Herbert 71
Menkler family 38
Menuez, Bernice 24
Menuez, Rollin 24
Meyer, Ben 120
Miller, Aden 46, 47

ABOUT THE AUTHORS

A graduate of Miami and Ohio State Universities, DAVID MEYERS has written a number of local histories, as well as works for the stage and several novels, including *Hello, I Must Be Going: The Mostly True Story of an Imaginary Band*. David was recently inducted into the Ohio Senior Citizens Hall of Fame for his contributions to local history.

ELISE MEYERS WALKER is a graduate of Hofstra University and Ohio University. She has collaborated with her father on a dozen local histories, including *Ohio's Black Hand Syndicate, Lynching and Mob Violence in Ohio*, and *Historic Black Settlements of Ohio*. They are both available for presentations.

The authors' website is www.explodingstove.com, or readers can follow them on Twitter, YouTube, Facebook and Instagram @explodingstove.